# Naturally Healthy

## A Vegetarian Guide to Wholesome Eating and Cooking

### PHILIPPA ANNETT

Illustrations by Billie Fincham

KAYE & WARD
KINGSWOOD

COLOUR PLATES

Colour plates appear between pages:
34 and 35
66 and 67
98 and 99
130 and 131

All photography by John Barrett
except for picture opposite page 131 by Anthony Blake

Text copyright © 1984 by Philippa Annett

Index compiled by Isobel McLean

Published by Kaye & Ward Ltd
The Windmill Press, Kingswood, Tadworth, Surrey
1984

ISBN 0 7182 1570 2

Printed in Great Britain at the
University Press, Cambridge
from typesetting by
Alacrity Phototypesetters
Banwell Castle, Weston-super-Mare

# Contents

The recipes in the text in *italics* with an * can be found under relevant section headings.

*For my loved ones,*
*whose continued enthusiasm, encouragement and shared interest*
*in this book helped so much to make it possible.*

# Introduction

Today in the western world, more and more people realize that we are suffering increasingly from ill health due to poor diet. Overweight and undernourished, we are the end products of starch and sugar excesses, and of convenience foods which have been refined, processed and dyed until stripped of most of their original nutrients. As a result, there is a growing interest in an alternative healthier way of eating.

A truly healthy diet is one that obtains maximum benefit from foods that are whole, natural and unrefined: foods rich in the nutritional value of protein, vitamins and minerals, and free from the chemical additives used in the production of so many of today's foods. Its rewards are an increased physical and mental vitality, and a radiant good health, because the food we eat determines what we are.

A new way of eating is not undertaken lightly by anyone, and breaking a lifetime of bad eating habits hardly happens overnight, so perhaps the change-over should be gradual! But it is everyday eating that is so important and while at first that 'craved for', banished treat may still be occasionally enjoyed, for the rest of the time explore a diet that is full of the goodness of fresh fruit, vegetables and wholefoods. And when you've sampled the marvellous flavours of wholesome natural foods, and delighted in the clear skin and eyes, shining hair and vibrant energy that accompanies good health, any craving for unhealthy foods will gradually cease, and there'll be no stopping you!

I have concentrated on an entirely meatless diet, for the benefit of both those already confirmed vegetarians, and (on the proven basis that most people eat too much meat for their own good) those just wanting to supplement their diet with economical and tasty meatless meals that are rich in all the vital nutrients of life. There is an abundance of natural health-giving foods available to us, and I hope that this book will give help and encouragement towards discovering and utilizing some of them, as well as proving that a healthier diet can and ought to be enjoyed by everyone.

## FOOD FOR THOUGHT

It is a fact recognized by anyone interested in healthy foods, that we need to eat more raw vegetables and fruit as a main part of our diet. The cooking of these foods so easily destroys not only valuable vitamins and minerals, but also digestive enzymes, and for this reason every meal ideally should be started with, or at least contain, something raw and fresh. Full of digestion aiding enzymes, this will stimulate the gastric juices and help the body to digest and utilize protein more fully.

In fact most foods, apart from some starches, are healthier eaten raw. Because their protein, vitamin and mineral content, as well as the digestive enzymes they contain, have not been diminished by cooking, raw foods are in consequence of far higher nutritional value, while being more easily and completely digested. Protein foods particularly (with the obvious exception of pulses!*) are more fully absorbed when eaten uncooked, and milk, cheese and nuts should be eaten raw as often as possible.

* Dried peas, beans and lentils

The choice of whether or not to eat meat for whatever reason must be a personal one. But on our overcrowded planet, life saving, body building protein is precious. Millions are starving, and yet vast amounts of protein-rich grain and seed are fed to cattle and pigs. It takes about 20 lbs of vegetable protein to produce only 1 lb of meat, and at the time of writing, about 24,000 animals are slaughtered for meat each working day in Britain alone!

But it may also be as well to recognize some other facts about meat as a source of protein in a healthy diet. As the consumption rate of meat, eaten in the affluent west as the prime source of protein, has risen with our standard of living, so has the percentage of digestive complaints, heart attacks and cancer, and questions inevitably must be asked as to the advisability of including flesh foods in a healthy diet.

One possible answer might be that because cooking destroys essential digestive enzymes in all foods, cooked meat cannot be completely broken down by the digestive system. In effect, the more cooking meat is subjected to, the more indigestible it becomes, and it turns in consequence to waste matter of the type, and in the quantities, that the body cannot get rid of quickly enough. This retained, semi-digested protein waste becomes toxic in the bowel, and the bloodstream becomes unclean and poisoned.

Another health hazard, which could arise today from the eating of flesh foods and processed animal products, is the inclusion of many unnatural additives. Animals factory-bred for eating are often treated with hormones to fatten them, while processed animal and dairy products undergo treatment with chemical preservatives. The eating of these foods results in the clogging of the body cells with chemicals, hormones, excess salt and other food additives.

So although it may be advisable to omit flesh foods from the healthy diet, at least on a regular basis, if the need is felt for meat, avoid all factory-bred and processed meats; choose in preference naturally reared animals, wildfowl, or fish. Eggs should be free range, cheeses natural and unprocessed, and yoghurt is healthier eaten 'live'. And all protein foods, including cooked meat, are more easily and completely digested if eaten with green leafy vegetables, preferably raw in salad combinations or only very lightly cooked.

With the excessive consumption of meat and processed foods, together with chemical additives which are used in the production of so much, and no-value foods such as sugar and white refined cereal, it is hardly surprising that our digestive systems cease to be efficient. Food and toxic products remain far too long as waste matter in the intestines, and the many germs and viruses that thrive on waste products in the body are more likely to survive. In this way poor diet and the resulting contamination and poisoning of the bloodstream probably contribute to the many digestive disorders, diseases and viruses so prevalent today.

It is therefore essential to good health that enough roughage is eaten every day to encourage efficient passage of waste products from the body, and to ensure a clean unpoisoned bloodstream, a clear skin and greater vitality. Foods containing roughage, such as whole grain, pulses, nuts, raw vegetables and fruit, should constitute a major part of the healthy diet.

# Small Beginnings

Embarking on a healthier way of eating is begun by replacing certain undesirable everyday foods with natural, healthy and nutritious alternatives. This can of course be done immediately by the very adventurous, but it will be more economical if current foods are allowed to run out before being discarded from the diet. And that way too the family is given a little time to get used to new tastes!

## SUGAR

All sugar, whether brown or white, is unnecessary, and excess is poisonous. It contains only calories which lead to weight gain, and has no nutritional value at all. It is acid forming, tooth decaying and, most importantly, overloads the pancreas and reduces the body's capacity to utilize protein, vitamins and minerals, leading inevitably to ill health. Heart disease and diabetes have been connected with sugar consumption. Sufficient sugar is in fact produced for the body's needs from the natural digestion of fruit, vegetables and grain, and the consumption of refined sugar and sugared products can be reduced considerably by replacing them with natural ingredients:

**Honey** is a gentle, predigested and completely natural sweetener. It contains vitamins, minerals, and digestion aiding enzymes and, like sugar, produces instant energy. Spread golden honey on your bread instead of jam or marmalade, and use a thinner honey to replace sugar in cooking. But it is worth noting that a little less honey than sugar is needed, and any liquid in the recipe should be slightly reduced. Most good health food shops sell honey in bulk at a reasonable price, and all honeys available there will be unprocessed and contain maximum nutrients.

**Molasses** is another natural sweetener and exceptionally rich in B vitamins, iron and other minerals. But because of a strong taste, it is probably best used only for cooking, and very sparingly.

A little **Raw Cane** or **Maple** sugar can be used occasionally. Although all sugar is undesirable, genuine raw sugar is less refined and possibly retains some natural mineral content. Use in moderation as an alternative sweetener.

Fresh fruit, yoghurt and cheese make delicious and healthy puddings, but for an occasional treat, home-made puddings, cakes, biscuits and even ice cream can be produced from natural ingredients giving some nutritional value with controlled sugar content.

In place of sweets and chocolates, try chewing on raw dried fruit, again available in bulk from health food shops. Dried apricots, apple rings, bananas, peaches, pears and raisins will satisfy a sweet tooth while being an excellent source of nutrition. And to replace sugared squashes and 'fizzy' drinks, have freshly prepared or diluted unsweetened fruit juices.

## CEREALS

For centuries man lived on whole grain; natural, protective and more kind to the digestive system, it provided maximum protein, vitamin and mineral supply. His bread was made from the whole grain, stone ground into flour; flour which included the valuable outer coating of bran, and the nutritious wheatgerm, both of which are so vital to good health.

But modern refinement and milling processes remove the bran and the germ from the grain, and in so doing destroy most of the B vitamins and protein in our flour and cereal products. White bread, instant breakfast cereals, and white spaghetti or macaroni on supermarket shelves today are not the sustaining and nutritious foods they ought to be. And white rice is a polished inferior substitute to the natural, brown and highly nourishing cereal from which it is processed.

To replace these modern health hazards, seek out whole grain cereals and their products. Higher in protein, B vitamins and minerals, these foods are unrefined, natural and very much tastier:
**Stone-ground Whole Grain Flour** for all cooking purposes.
**Wholemeal Bread** an excellent source of calcium, iron, B vitamins, vitamin E, and some protein; an invaluable food.
**Wholemeal Pasta** most types can be bought made from wholemeal flour.
**Whole Brown Rice** which is available in many different varieties.
**Whole Cereal Grains** that have been cracked, flaked or rolled to make them more digestible and easier to prepare or cook, and which can be home-made into delicious breakfast cereals to replace commercial refined varieties.

## ANIMAL FATS

All animal fats, such as butter, lard, dripping and some margarines, are saturated fats, the eating of which leads to a rise in the level of cholesterol in the blood. Too much cholesterol is dangerous. It can result in a hardening of the arteries, and is a contributory factor of heart attacks and coronary thrombosis.

Sunflower or safflower oil margarines are preferable substitutes for butter, and likewise sunflower or safflower oils, 'cold pressed' and 'unhydrogenated', should be used if possible for cooking as well as for salads. These two vegetable oils are especially high in polyunsaturates which help fight the cholesterol battle and lower the risk of heart attacks; soya oil, sesame oil, corn oil and olive oil are also good substitutes. Keep the cholesterol level down further by avoiding cream, whole milk and cream cheese, and beware of the cholesterol-high ingredients of all commercial cakes, pastries, biscuits, ice creams, chocolate and puddings; eat low fat yoghurt instead of cream and custards, use powdered skim milk or plant milk instead of whole milk, and choose low fat cheeses. If eating meat, eat only lean meats, but even these irregularly.

## SALT

Sea salt should be used in preference to other table salts because of its high natural mineral content. But although salt is essential to the human body, when taken in excess it is very harmful to health. Unless living in a very hot climate or doing heavy manual work, and consequently losing a lot of body salt through perspiration, the amount of salt needed by the body is little compared to the amount most people consume. Sufficient natural sodium, present in salt and necessary to the human body, will be obtained from a balanced diet of other foods, and excess can lead to ill health. There is salt enough added to all commercially prepared foods to preserve them, including bread, butter, cheese and food flavourings such as yeast extracts, stock cubes and tomato purée, to make the addition of much more inadvisable. With the minimum of salt added to food in cooking or at the table, the palate is very quickly educated to like less salt, and the delicate flavours of fresh herbs could be rediscovered as a substitute in savoury recipes.

# The Vital Nutrients of Life

## PROTEIN

Essential for growth, repair, vitality and life, protein must make up a proportion of the food we eat daily.

Many cereal grains, pulses, nuts, seeds and vegetables are so rich in protein as well as vitamins and minerals, that with a balanced diet of these, meat is not only unnecessary, but wasteful and not particularly healthy. Together with dairy products, these nutritious foods can be used to replace meat in a vegetarian diet. Protein is made up of a collection of essential amino acids. Complete protein foods (meat, fish and dairy products) are those which contain all these amino acids. Incomplete protein foods (pulses, whole cereal grains, nuts and seeds) are rich in some of the amino acids and poor in others. But, because each type of incomplete protein food has a different distribution of amino acids, by combining one type with another at the same meal, or with a high-value complete protein food such as eggs, cheese, milk or yoghurt, they can be made to complement each other and wonderfully complete protein nutrition is created. It is complete protein that is needed for body building purposes, and combinations of these protein foods, which I have put to complementary effect for the recipes in this book, can result in meals which contain as much if not more complete protein value as a meat meal.

Listed below are the main sources of vegetarian protein foods:

**Dairy Foods**
Dairy foods are rich in complete high-value protein. In other words they contain all the essential amino acids in balanced proportions needed for body building. They also supply some vitamin B12 absent from most other vegetarian foods. B12 tablets could be taken occasionally to supplement this deficiency. By combining dairy products with a whole cereal food such as a slice of wholemeal bread or a serving of rice or pasta, the value of both foods is increased and, because a certain amount of starch aids protein absorption, the starch content of the cereal is put to good use. But the amount of starch need only be minimal unless feeding athletes! Alternatively, a serving of vegetables, such as potatoes, parsnips, broad beans or peas, provides the required small amount of starch.
Types include:

| | |
|---|---|
| Cheese | A good source of complete protein which also contains vitamin A, some of the B vitamins, and calcium. Lovely for children especially. Cheese is even supposed to have some natural penicillin in it! However, it has a rather high animal fat and salt content, and can be replaced by cottage cheese if required. |
| Cottage Cheese | An excellent low fat and low calorie, complete protein food, with all the vitamins and minerals of hard cheese. |
| Milk | A very good source of calcium also vitamins A, K and some B vitamins. Milk is an easily absorbed, complete protein food. |
| Skim Milk Powder | Without the fat and calorific content of whole milk, skim milk powder is a concentrated high-value source of protein. |
| Yoghurt | Should ideally be eaten regularly to benefit |

from its almost magical reputation of health giving properties. A superb protein food.

Eggs      Contain a wealth of goodness as well as being a most biologically balanced complete protein food, with vitamins A, D, E, some B vitamins, calcium and iron.

## Pulses

These are an excellent source of protein, and contain B vitamins and iron. There are many different kinds of dried peas and beans, the most nutritious of them being soya beans, followed closely by chick peas. Soya beans especially contain more protein value than meat and, in addition, contain vitamin E, calcium and other vital minerals. Because the starch content of peas and beans is fairly low and the fat content minimal, pulses also have a very favourable nutritional-to-calorific value.

To complete the protein value of pulses, combine with a cereal or with nuts, and serve with vegetables to provide vitamin A and vitamin C.

Types include:

Soya Beans      Including soya products such as soya flour, soya splits or grits, which are toasted pieces of soya, all valuable food additives to boost protein. And soya sauce (Shoyu or Tamari) is useful for adding flavour to savoury food.

Chick Peas

Lentils

Split Peas      And other varieties of dried peas.

Beans      All varieties.

To cook:

Most pulses need soaking overnight in cold water, if possible in the fridge, after being thoroughly washed. The length of time soaking reduces the cooking they need. Add salt, and then bring to the boil in the same water, which will contain nutrients from the beans, and simmer until tender. This will take 1-2 hours, and sometimes much more, depending on the type and age of the bean. Lentils and split peas need little or no soaking — a couple of hours maybe — and will be tender any time after half and hour's cooking. The tiny red Egyptian lentils can be cooked straight away.

## Nuts and Seeds

Rich in B vitamins and minerals, nuts and seeds are a very concentrated, high protein food, and only a few are needed to make a meal. Sunflower seeds deserve special mention as they have a superb food content, yet their nutritional-to-calorific value is more favourable to weight watchers than that of some other nuts. Sesame seeds too are full of protein, vitamins and minerals, and you can buy a nourishing sesame seed paste called Tahini which can be used in a number of ways. Combine nuts and seeds with a pulse food or whole cereal product to complete the protein value. But a mixture of different kinds of nuts and seeds will also provide complete protein nutrition, and a handful of nuts, seeds and raisins followed maybe by some yoghurt or fresh fruit, makes an excellent quick snack for that reason. Accompany meals made of nuts and seeds with vegetables to provide vitamins A and C; a dairy product could be served at the same meal to provide extra calcium.

Types include:

| | |
|---|---|
| Sunflower Seeds | Full of protein, B vitamins, vitamin E, iron, calcium and minerals. |
| Sesame Seeds | Excellent source of iron, calcium and protein. |
| Peanuts | Including peanut butter, both good sources of B vitamins and protein; especially valuable for children. |
| Pine Kernels | |
| Almonds | |
| Hazelnuts | |
| Walnuts | |
| Brazil Nuts | Very nutritious, but calorific value rather higher than other nuts. |
| Cashew Nuts | So good, but these nuts have a high cholesterol content. |

**N.B.** With the exception of cashew nuts, most nuts and seeds contain a low proportion of cholesterol.

## Whole Grain Cereals

Essential for good health, whole grain cereals provide protein, vital B vitamins and vitamin E, as well as calcium, iron and other valuable minerals. Whole grain cereals can be bought from all good health food shops, either cracked, rolled or flaked for convenience, or stone ground into flour.

To complete the protein value of cereals, combine with pulses, seeds or nuts, or eat with a complete protein dairy product for greater food value.

Types include:

| | |
|---|---|
| Wheat | Made into wholewheat products such as wholemeal bread, wholemeal flour (stone ground), wheatgerm and bran, wholemeal pasta and semolina. |
| Oats | Made into oatmeal. Possibly the most nutritious of the cereals, full of vitamins, minerals and protein. |
| Millet | Has a very good protein and vitamin B content, and contains little starch. |
| Barley | An easily digestible, light cereal. |
| Rye | Dark, nutritious and with a deliciously nutty flavour. |
| Brown Rice | A very nourishing cereal, and easy to overeat! But not much is needed to make up excellent food value while avoiding excess calorific content. |

To cook:

Whole or cracked grains can be cooked and served like rice (see page 116) to make delicious savoury grain dishes; flaked grains soaked overnight and cooked in milk or a milk and water mixture, can be served as porridge with milk or yoghurt, honey and fruit (see breakfast recipes).

## CARBOHYDRATES

Carbohydrates are needed to provide energy and warmth and, when the diet is based on whole and natural foods, they can be valuable sources of vitamins, minerals, protein and vital roughage. The main sources are:

| | |
|---|---|
| Sugars | All sugars, refined and natural, and including honey and molasses. |
| | Fruits, some containing more natural sugar than others. |
| | Dried fruit. |
| Starches | Cereal products. |
| | Pulses. |
| | Some vegetables such as potatoes, peas and beans. |

## FATS

Fats are used with carbohydrates to provide energy and warmth, and are also needed in the body to enable the fat-soluble vitamins (A, D, E and K) to be properly absorbed.
The main sources are:
Butter and margarine
Vegetable, cooking and salad oils
Hard cheese
Cream
Whole milk
Nuts
Egg yolk

Animal fats are not advisable for cholesterol, acidic and general health reasons, and should be replaced by vegetable oils and margarine. But as the digestibility of all fats is adversely effected by cooking, it is preferable to use only a minimum amount in cooking.

Too much fat in any form is bad for the health, skin and figure, and the quantity eaten of fats or oils, and fatty foods, is best limited. As already suggested, high-fat whole milk can be replaced very nutritiously by skim milk powder, high fat cheeses by cottage cheese, and cream by yoghurt.

It is, incidentally, a good idea to eat some form of starch with fats, as this ensures the easier digestion of the fat. This also applies to the eating of fatty foods. For example, always have a slice of wholemeal bread or crispbread with hard cheese, and even whole milk is better digested if accompanied with bread or cereals.

## VITAMINS

**Main Sources**

**Vitamin A** Helps protect against infection, and is essential for healthy skin, hair and nails and for protecting the eyes and respiratory organs. Also needed for the healthy development of bones and teeth. Vitamin A is destroyed by bright light.

Milk, Skim milk powder, Plant milk, Cheeses, Eggs, Vegetable margarine, Butter, Wheatgerm oil, Apricots and figs, Prunes, Tomatoes, Carrots, Lettuce, Spinach, Broccoli, Kale, Dandelion, Parsley, Watercress.

**Vitamin B** The vitamin B complex contains many different factors, all of which work together and control the utilization of protein, carbo-hydrates and fats. Essential for the sound functioning of the nervous system and to maintain vitality. Water soluble, the B vitamins can be partially destroyed by cooking, storing and modern food processing methods.

Brewers yeast, Yeast extract, Food yeast, Soya beans and soya products, Wheatgerm, Whole grains, Oatmeal, Brown rice, Wholemeal bread, Peanuts and peanut butter, Walnuts, Brazil nuts, Almonds, Sunflower seeds, Sesame seeds, Beans, Bean sprouts, Peas, Lentils, Avocados, Most leafy green vegetables, Dandelions, Leeks, Potatoes, Pumpkins, Carrots, Swedes, Mushrooms,

23

Tomatoes, Yoghurt, Skim milk powder, Milk, Vitamin enriched plant milk, Buttermilk, Eggs, Cheese, Cottage cheese, Melon, Grapes, Prunes, Dates, Molasses.

**Vitamin C** Increases resistance to infection, assists healing of wounds and recovery after illness, and is needed for the absorption of other vitamins and minerals. Must be taken daily as the body cannot store vitamin C. As well as being soluble in water, this vitamin is very easily destroyed by exposure to air, light and heat.

Citrus fruits: *Oranges, Lemons, Grapefruits,* Pineapples, Most green leafy vegetables, Cabbage, Sprouts, Watercress, Parsley, Dandelions, Most wild berries, Black and Red currants, Strawberries, Raspberries, Blackberries, Gooseberries, Rosehips, Melons, Tomatoes, Peas, Potatoes, Peppers, Cauliflower.

**Vitamin D** Helps in the absorption of minerals, especially calcium. Necessary for healthy bones and teeth, particularly in childhood.

Eggs, Sunflower seeds, Vitaminized vegetable margarine. Also absorbed from sunlight. N.B. Vegetarians will obtain sufficient vitamin D from the above foods, but children might benefit from a vitamin D supplement in the winter.

| | | |
|---|---|---|
| **Vitamin E** | Necessary for normal growth and development, and to help the body utilize vitamin A. Lack of this vitamin leads to problems and diseases of the circulation. Still something of a mystery, vitamin E is also supposed to be beneficial to the muscular tissue and the nervous system, and is sometimes called the 'youth vitamin'; it is said that a deficiency shows up as brown 'liver spots' on the skin. | Whole grains, Wholemeal bread, Eggs, Seeds, Nuts, Soya beans and soya oil, Wheatgerm and wheatgerm oil, Watercress. |
| **Vitamin K** | Vital for the normal clotting of the blood. | Green leafy vegetables, Cauliflower, Green peas, Soya oil, Egg yolk. |

## MINERALS

**Main sources**

| | | |
|---|---|---|
| **Calcium** | Necessary for the formation and preservation of strong bones and teeth. Also needed to ensure proper functioning of the blood and muscles. | Skim milk powder, Milk, Yoghurt, Cheese, Eggs, Green leafy vegetables, Oats. Almonds, Sunflower seeds, Sesame seeds, Soya flour, Soya products, Dried apricots, Wholemeal flour and bread, Wheatgerm. |

| | | |
|---|---|---|
| **Iron** | Essential for healthy blood and vitality. Needed in increased quantities by teenagers of both sexes and by women, especially during pregnancy. | Eggs, Pulses, Soya flour, Wholemeal flour and bread, Whole grains, Wheatgerm, Oatmeal, Dried fruits: *Apricots, Peaches, Dates, Raisins.* Yeast, Yeast extracts, Molasses, Sunflower and Sesame seeds, Nuts: *Almonds, Peanuts, Cashew, Walnuts,* Prune juice, Leafy green vegetables. |

**Phosphorus Potassium Magnesium Sodium Iodine Zinc Copper** Are among other vital minerals necessary for the normal functioning of the body. But because these are all widely distributed among so many common foods, there is little chance of having a deficiency of any of these minerals, especially with a diet of wholesome and natural foods.

# A Plan of Healthy Eating

In planning a healthy, well balanced diet, all the nutrients needed by the body for complete health must be included in the day's meals:

| | |
|---|---|
| **Protein** | Complete protein found in dairy products or combined vegetable protein products, i.e. nuts, seeds, pulses and whole cereals. |
| **Vitamins** (especially the B vitamins) **and Minerals** | These will be supplied by eating a varied range of protein and carbohydrate foods together with plenty of fresh fruit and fresh green and yellow vegetables, at *least* half the daily intake eaten raw. And a daily amount of whole-grain cereals including wholemeal bread is a must in a healthy diet. |

27

**Starch Foods** Chosen discriminately, starches in a whole food diet are useful sources of vitamins, minerals and protein as well as roughage. If weight watching though, the amount of starch foods eaten must obviously be controlled. (See Weight Watching on a Wholefood Diet.)

**Sugars** Refined sugar and all sugared products ought to be avoided wherever possible, and replaced with honey and other natural ingredients if and when needed.

**Fats** Fat content ideally should be kept to a minimum in the diet, and that eaten should consist mainly of vegetable rather than animal fats.

But, in fact, by eating a wide variety of whole, natural and healthy foods, carefully prepared and cooked to preserve maximum nutritive value, and plenty of fresh fruit and vegetables, there should never be any protein, vitamin or mineral deficiency.

## AMONG VALUABLE FOODS

Although no one food can supply on its own all the necessary nutrients, there are nevertheless some foods which have exceptional value one way or another, and it is very beneficial to include regularly these goodly foods in a plan of healthy eating.

**Yoghurt** Eaten daily live and natural, either on its own, or as a salad dressing or recipe addition, or honey-sweetened for a perfect pudding, yoghurt in some form is a must in any healthy diet. Yoghurt is high in complete and predigested protein, and it contains lactic acid which aids the absorption of protein, calcium and iron. Eaten regularly, yoghurt also produces B vitamins and vitamin K in the intestines, and helps destroy harmful bacteria in the digestive tract.

The best way to ensure a regular supply of this invaluable food is to make your own, and by far the easiest method of doing this is to invest in a home yoghurt maker. The initial, marginal, expense involved is soon more than paid off by the amount saved on bought yoghurt! Instructions supplied with the yoghurt maker involve mixing yoghurt starter with about 2 pints of milk, pouring it into the containers, switching on, and leaving for about 8 hours or overnight until set. I have produced the best results by using either skim milk powder, made with an extra tablespoon or two of milk powder to obtain a very good low fat, high protein yoghurt, or Longlife milk which produces very creamy textured yoghurt.

**Skim Milk Powder** Skim milk powder is an excellent source of high-value complete protein, calcium, vitamin A and the B vitamins, while being low in calories, carbohydrate and fat. Perfect for slimmers or for those on a low fat diet, powdered milk is also ideal used in cooking to boost the nutritional and protein content of many recipes. Buy if possible from health food shops.

**Cottage or Curd Cheese** Also very good protein foods, containing all the goodness of hard cheese without the calorie and fat content. To be sure of no unwanted additives, making your own curd cheese from yoghurt is very easy (see recipes) and well worth doing as it can be put to so many uses.

**Wheatgerm** Wheatgerm, the embryo of the wheat grain, is exceptionally high in the B vitamins and vitamin E, and a good source of iron and calcium. A valuable and nutritious protein food.

Buy 'natural' wheatgerm from health food shops in preference to the more commercial 'stabilized' wheatgerm, which has been treated to last longer. Natural wheatgerm ought to be stored in a cool dark place.

It is delicious sprinkled on cereals, added to muesli, mixed with yoghurt and honey or added to pastry, cakes or bread mixtures.

**Bran Roughage** Roughage is vital to ensure completion of the digestive process, and it is a serious lack of roughage in the modern refined diet that constitutes a major health problem. Although sufficient roughage should be obtained naturally in a health food diet from whole cereal foods, pulses, nuts and raw fruit and vegetables, additional roughage can be eaten if necessary in the form of bran. Bran is the outer coating of the wheat grain, removed with the germ during modern milling processes, and provides roughage as well as containing B vitamins and some protein. Bran or a bran cereal is very good sprinkled over breakfast cereals or added to bread or cake recipes.

**Brewers Yeast** Contains complete high-value protein and is rich in iron and the B vitamins, including the all too rare vitamin B12. Brewers yeast can be taken in pill form, used in cooking or, if you like the taste, just sprinkled on breakfast cereal. Yeast extracts, such as Marmite, used often in cooking are an ideal alternative way of consuming brewers yeast, providing excellent flavour as well as food value to many savoury recipes.

**Dried Fruit** All dried fruits are rich in protein, vitamins and minerals, and should be eaten regularly in their raw state. Containing all the goodness of the fresh fruit in a concentrated form, available dried fruits include raisins, currants and sultanas, dates, figs, prunes, apricots, peaches, pears, bananas and apples. Apricots especially are a valuable source of vitamin A, calcium, iron, and they contain some protein. Dried apricots and apples also retain a good vitamin C content. Eaten in their raw state both make tasty chewy snacks and as their calorific value is less than that of other dried fruits, they're kinder on the figure too. (Though eaten in moderation, of course!)

To ensure that they have not been chemically treated, buy all dried fruit from health food shops, where you can usually obtain made-up packs of mixed dried fruits too. But the fruits will need washing before eating. To plump up dried fruits without subjecting them to cooking, cover such fruits as figs, prunes, apricots, peaches, pears, bananas, apples and raisins with boiling water and add a little honey. (1 teaspoon molasses added to prunes as well gives a delicious flavour to the juice.) Leave to soak overnight and eat with breakfast cereal or as a pudding accompanied with honey-sweetened yoghurt. Prunes have the added bonus of being a natural laxative while containing few calories. Ideal for slimmers!

**Bananas** Bananas are an easy to digest, high-value food. They contain some easily absorbed protein, vitamins A and C, and have a low content of fat, cholesterol, sodium and calories, making them ideal for many special diets. Because of their acid-neutralizing properties, bananas are gentle on the digestive system, and consequently are of great value for those with any digestive or intestinal disorders. Coming ready-wrapped in a protective skin, and always available, these are a marvellous natural 'convenience' food.

**Avocados** These luxurious fruits are rich in protein and B vitamins, and also contain vitamins A, C, D and E. An excellent value, low-calorie and -carbohydrate food.

**Watercress** Watercress is very rich in minerals and vitamins A, E and C and is a most valuable food for keeping the blood healthy.

**Parsley** Containing iron and vitamins A and C, parsley is regarded by herbalists as an inner cleanser. At any rate it is an invaluable herb for adding flavour, and if you've been eating garlic, chewing on some raw fresh parsley will help to remove any odour!

**Dandelions** A useful addition to salads, dandelion leaves collected from the garden contain some essential minerals and vitamins A and C as well as some of the B vitamins. Good for the elimination of water retention, they are also said to be beneficial to the liver. Choose young leaves for a salad. Dandelion-root coffee (available from health food shops) is surprisingly good and, being rich in minerals, is far better for you than coffee from beans.

**Garlic** Garlic has always been regarded highly as having many remedial and medicinal qualities. It is a natural antiseptic and is very good for the digestive system while, among other attributes, it reduces body catarrh and lowers blood pressure. It certainly adds a whole lot of unbeatable flavour to cooking and salads and, in fact, is mostly detected on the breath if eaten raw.

**Bean Sprouts** The protein, vitamin and mineral value of beans or seeds is vastly increased when they are sprouted. All beans, seeds

31

and even grain can be sprouted by washing them in warm water, soaking them overnight, and then keeping them moist in a warm place. After a few days they should have sprouted, and when the shoots are an inch or so in length they can add extra taste and nourishment to a green salad. Mung beans (Chinese bean sprouts) are also delicious lightly cooked in a little oil, water and soya sauce, and can sometimes be bought ready sprouted. Sprouting packs are available from many health food shops or seed suppliers, together with full instructions on how to grow them. Varieties include alfalfa, aduki beans and fenugreek, and many others are available.

**Apple Cider Vinegar** Deserves a special mention under this heading because of the many and varied healing qualities it possesses. Rich in minerals, and greatly superior to all other vinegars, cider vinegar regulates the acid/alkaline balance in the body and is wonderfully healthy and therapeutic for the whole digestive tract and allied organs. It is also a very good tonic for the blood; and because of its antiseptic qualities, apple cider vinegar makes an excellent gargle, using 1 teaspoon in a glass of warm water and swallowing some of the liquid.

Use in salad dressings or make a drink of this healing liquid by diluting 2 teaspoons of the vinegar in a glass of water and sweetening with a little honey. Be sure to buy cider vinegar which states on the label that it is made from whole apples. A mixture of apple cider vinegar and honey, called Honeygar, can be bought too.

**Plant Milk** Belongs in this section really only because it is a very useful food for vegans (vegetarians who also exclude all dairy products from their diet) or for those who cannot take cows' milk. Plant milk is made from soya, and is available from health food shops, either dried, cartoned, or canned. It is rich in protein and free from animal fat and cholesterol.

**Instant Vegetarian Protein Foods** Textured vegetable protein (TVP) made from soya can be bought either minced or in chunks from health food shops. A highly nutritious substitute for meat, TVP needs only to be hydrated by soaking or boiling in water for a short time before using like meat to form the basis of some very tasty main meal dishes. And being very much cheaper than meat, it is a useful, economical and convenient food for meat eaters and vegetarians alike. There are also other types of soya, cereal or nut based, packeted protein foods on the market. Produced by a number of different manufacturers and available at most health food shops, these serve to provide quick emergency meals when needed, and it's always useful to have a packet in the cupboard. Manufacturers supply full preparation and cooking instructions and many include some handy recipe ideas too.

## WEIGHT WATCHING
## ON A WHOLEFOOD DIET

It is of course as possible to maintain or lose weight on a wholefood diet as it is on a meat eating one. The protein-to-calorific value of cereals, pulses or nuts when served as the *main* source of protein in a meal (as opposed to extras in a meat meal or nibbles between) compares very well with that of other types of food. Successful weight watching on any type of diet need only primarily involve keeping an eye on quantities and, when eating a vegetarian diet or wholesome and natural foods as recommended in this book, the rules for would-be slimmers are no different.

People basically gain weight when they eat carbohydrates, fats and protein in excess of their body's needs, so in order to lose weight, the quantities of these nutrients must be controlled:

Cut right down on obvious starches such as cakes, biscuits and puddings, and that extra piece of bread or second helping of potatoes. But the quality of starch foods eaten in a weight watcher's diet is important. While foods such as cakes and biscuits contain just high-calorie starch with little or no food value, many starches in a whole food diet are extremely nutritious, containing a wide variety of protein, vitamins or minerals needed for good health. It can be therefore ill-advised for the health-conscious weight watcher to cut out high-value starch foods completely.

Replace puddings with fresh fruit or yoghurt (healthier too for everyone), and make it easier on yourself by not restocking the biscuit tin! You'll be doing everyone a favour, and children will benefit by having wholemeal toast and honey or a piece of fruit for their tea-time snack instead.

Keep fats and cooking or salad oils in the diet to a minimum, and frequent use of such foods as skim milk powder, cottage or curd cheese, low fat yoghurt and eggs will greatly help would-be slimmers as they are all excellent high value protein foods with low calorie and fat content.

To start the day, the perfect breakfast for slimmers and others is a bowl of *Swiss Muesli** (see recipes). It's full of energy-giving goodness which will last you throughout the morning. So too is the *Fruit and Yoghurt Breakfast** while a bowl of yoghurt or a boiled egg, either one accompanied with a piece of wholemeal toast and honey, or a refreshing all fruit breakfast makes a healthy change.

One meal a day could be a simple salad meal. Have one of the complete-meal protein salads from the recipes, or prepare any salad combination and accompany with some cottage cheese or a hard boiled egg. Make salads colourful and interesting, using plenty of different vegetables and fruit. Salads make excellent fillers, and can be eaten freely. But watch the amount of oil for dressing, and preferably use lemon juice, apple cider vinegar or a yoghurt dressing instead.

The main meal of the day should contain a sensible portion of any of the main meal recipes in this book, eaten with a generous selection of raw or lightly cooked vegetables. Complete the meal with some yoghurt or fresh fruit. A side salad, fruit or a light soup could also be served as a starter if you like; and in fact, chewing on something raw at the start of the meal not only helps the body digest other foods, but takes the edge off your appetite so that you eat less!

Eating to maintain or lose weight is a matter of getting into the right frame of mind. Those people who impose upon themselves strict regimented diet campaigns, and who are obsessed with every mouthful of food they eat, often become depressed and irritable by the rigidity of their diet. And it is not very surprising to know that

many of the strictest weight watchers have sessions of eating compulsively all the foods which they deny themselves for so long, and end up as they begin, unhappy and still possibly overweight.

The secret of weight watching then is to try and clear the mind of any food obsession. Calmly follow a sensible eating campaign that will re-educate your stomach and mind to asking for less food. Of course it helps to have some compelling interest or job in hand, or even a good book. With many people, when the mind is bored it seeks to fill itself through the stomach! But by just taking smaller portions, refusing seconds and avoiding starchy or sweet nibbles and snacks between meals, you will be creating some good basic slimming rules for your sensible eating campaign. There obviously will be days when you eat a bit too much, or occasionally succumb to a craving, but don't panic! Just enjoy those times (provided they don't happen too often!) and try and cut down the next day. It helps to realize that sometimes a craving reflects a genuine need of the body for a certain food, which is why it is so important to have a varied and healthy diet. Remember that you are starting new eating habits that could keep you slim and healthy for a lifetime, and in making sure that the food eaten is of high value, the appetite is more satisfactorily appeased and the body will not lose out on any vital nutrients.

But although new eating habits are not acquired overnight, with patience and understanding your sensible eating campaign will gradually become habitual. And by making wholesome, healthy and natural foods your basis, weight can be lost and then very successfully maintained, while at the same time health, vitality and beauty are increased.

And when your desired weight is reached you can afford to add a few treats to your new sensible eating habits for, with a pair of scales as a guide, you can always keep in shape without ever having to do more than keep an eye on quantities!

# *Healthy Miscellanea*

The most important guide to a healthier way of eating must surely be knowledge, and experimenting with that should be fun. But the ultimate choice of the foods with which you choose to nourish yourself can only be up to you, for if we are at odds with our diet, we cannot feel at one with life. No two people are the same, and a uniform rigidity cannot be enjoyed or bring contentment. But by becoming more aware of the food you eat, of your nutritional needs and, through experimenting, of your personal likes and dislikes, you increase your knowledge. With that to guide you, you can then learn to heed the natural responses of your own body, and eat that which makes you, the individual, feel the best. This chapter may help to take that knowledge and understanding a little further.

Never eat to excess as this overloads the digestive system. It is a good idea to get up from the table with the feeling that more could be fitted in! And it takes about four and a half hours for a meal to digest, during which time it is kinder on the stomach if no other food is introduced.

Have plenty of sleep, fresh air and exercise. Some form of vigorous exercise should be taken each day.

Go easy on the coffee! Coffee contains caffeine, a stimulant which acts on the nervous system and increases the metabolic rate. Too much caffeine results in nervousness, high blood pressure and headaches, and although it can be helpful to take more B vitamins to compensate, it is better to drink coffee only in moderation. Decaffeinated coffee is free from stimulants but like all instant coffee it contains unnatural chemicals. It is probably more 'natural' to drink freshly ground coffee beans.

It is not very often realized that combining foods correctly is as important to good health as the foods themselves. Without getting too bogged down by details, this is basically because all foods need a different type of digestive condition in the stomach to be fully absorbed and utilized and if two vastly different such types of food are eaten at the same time, the proper digestion is adversely affected. For example, in order to get complete benefit from protein, the main protein meal should be accompanied by a minimum of excess starch, and should contain no animal fats, sugars or acid fruits, as these all restrict protein digestion. And all protein foods are better absorbed and utilized if eaten with plenty of raw or lightly cooked vegetables.

At the same time it is generally more advisable to keep the level of acidity in the body down, and to maintain an alkaline balance. Excess acidity, produced by eating acid-forming or wrongly combined foods, causes digestive discomfort and disorders, kidney and bladder troubles, headaches and general sluggishness. So in the ideal healthy diet the intake of acid-forming foods should be kept to a minimum and, as often as possible, foods that are incompatible with each other not combined. The main acid forming foods and incompatible food combinations are:

**Sugar**: is extremely acid forming and interferes with the digestion of other foods. It should be replaced by honey in moderation as a sweetener, and as suggested in the chapter 'Small Beginnings', naturally sweet products such as dried fruit can replace sweets and chocolates, and fresh fruit juices can replace sugared drinks.

**Sugar/Fruit Combinations:** sugar used in combination with any fruit, including jams and jellies, etc, results in excessive acidity, so honey must be used to sweeten fruit if necessary, and to replace jam.

**Sugar/Starch Mixtures:** such as cakes, biscuits and puddings etc, especially those made with refined sugar and white flour. But for that occasional treat, these can be made with less acidic results from more natural wholesome ingredients.

**Animal Fats:** contain a high level of cholesterol and for this reason are considered less healthy. They are acid-forming and retard the digestion of protein. Replace with polyunsaturated vegetable oils and margarine.

**Flesh Foods:** these are highly acid forming and are better left out of the diet. However, if eaten at all, accompany with vegetables which are alkaline forming.

**Fried and Fatty Foods:** the cooking of all fats and fatty foods renders them less digestible and more acidic, and frying any food increases its acidic results in the body. Generally speaking, the higher the fat content of food, the higher its acidic possibilities, but uncooked fatty foods, and vegetable oils eaten raw as in a salad dressing, are very much more readily digested and absorbed. But when any fat or fatty food is eaten without some accompanying starch food (see FATS page 22) it cannot be completely broken down by the digestive system, and the fat accumulates as toxic substances in the body.

**Acidic Fruits with Protein and Starches:** acidic fruits are generally the more sour fruits and include:

| | | |
|---|---|---|
| Oranges | Gooseberries | Red and blackcurrants |
| Lemons | Plums | Raspberries |
| Grapefruit | Rhubarb | Pineapple |

Although these are all excellent sources of vitamin C and should be included regularly in the healthy diet, acidic fruits produce the wrong conditions in the stomach for the proper digestion of protein and starch foods (except maybe nuts). Fruits of this type are probably best eaten or their juice drunk on their own, or with other fruits, vegetables or nuts. Meals that contain primarily protein and/or starch foods could be accompanied with sweet or semi-sweet fruits. Because many acid fruits are so bitter, they are often cooked with the addition of a sweetener. Cooking does in fact lower the acidic results, but they ought to be cooked quickly so as to preserve some vitamins and minerals, and honey is of course the best sweetener.

Semi-sweet fruits are comparatively low in digestion-restricting acid, and to a certain extent can be eaten with starch and protein foods fairly compatibly. These include:

| | |
|---|---|
| Apples | Peaches |
| Pears | Apricots |
| Grapes | Cherries |
| Melon | Greengages |
| Strawberries | Blackberries |

The sweet fruits contain no free acid and may be eaten freely with all other foods. These include:

| | |
|---|---|
| Dates | Raisins |
| Figs | Other dried fruits |
| Sultanas | Bananas |

**Sugar/Starch/Fruit Combinations:** such as fruit pies or crumbles, particularly those made with acidic fruits and including refined sugar and white flour! Also inadvisable are custards or sweet milk sauces with these fruits because of their protein as well as starch and sugar content. While starch/sugar/acidic fruit combinations are ideally best avoided, it could be argued that cooking lowers the acidic results of these fruits sufficiently for them to be combined more compatibly with a good starch food for that occasional treat! Better still, if really necessary, to use a less acid fruit such as apples for this kind of pudding and, when the temptation is strong, use honey to sweeten, a minimum amount of wholemeal flour or cereal for the topping, make a honey sweetened yoghurt sauce — and enjoy it!

All foods chewed well are kinder on the whole digestive system, and less is subsequently needed to satisfy the appetite. Saliva is alkaline which neutralizes acidity in the stomach.

# Equipment

There are a few basic pieces of kitchen equipment which make preparing wholefoods a lot simpler and quicker, and which are fairly essential in the making of many of the recipes.

For vegetables and salads, an extra-sharp knife comes in very useful; also a grater for both these and cheeses etc, either the old-fashioned handheld variety, or one which has a handle to turn and maybe various different sized revolving attachments. Some types are also able to attach to a surface. Alternatively, an electric grater does a marvellous grating job.

A liquidizer and food grinder combined is vital for such things as liquidizing soups, making smooth salad spreads and for grinding nuts and seeds. Kitchen scales, a measuring jug and a yoghurt maker are also among my most essential pieces of equipment, and others such as oven-to-table casseroles, a large flat sieve for draining and rinsing rice, and a food mixer are all put to good use. I also have a small food mill of the type used for mashing food for babies, which is put to many uses from mashing cooked beans to making apple purée, and I'd be lost without it.

# Metric Conversion

Recipe quantities are in imperial weights and measures, but these can be easily and successfully converted to metric if necessary, using the following conversion table. Figures are only approximate in order to make them easier to use, but provided recipes are completed in either imperial OR metric, this will not matter.

Weights to the nearest 25 grammes:

| 1oz | 25g |
|---|---|
| 4oz (¼lb) | 100g |
| 8oz (½lb) | 225g |
| 12oz (¾lb) | 350g |
| 16oz (1lb) | 450g |

Liquid measurements:

| 2floz | 50 millilitres |
|---|---|
| 5floz (¼ pint) | 150ml |
| 10floz (½ pint) | 300ml |
| ¾ pint | 450ml |
| 1 pint | 600ml |
| 1¾ pint | 1000ml (1 litre) |

# *Note to Readers*

All the recipes feed about 4 people unless otherwise stated.

The recipes shown in the text in *italics* with an * can be found under relevant section headings in this book.

It now only remains for me to hope that you enjoy experimenting with the recipes in this book as much as I did putting them together, and to wish you 'Bon Appetit'.

# *Breakfasts*

Breakfast should be considered a most important meal, and for the health food enthusiast does NOT consist of commercial, refined, breakfast cereal, a greasy platter of fried foods and white bread and butter! Instead, whole grain cereals flaked or rolled, oatmeal, wheatgerm, nuts, fresh fruit, yoghurt, honey and wholemeal bread or toast are all valuable ingredients for a wholesome and nutritious start to the day.

By far the most delicious and healthy breakfast food is *Swiss Muesli** which combines all the vital ingredients together: nutritious, wonderfully sustaining and excellent for the digestion, nerves and tissues. If you prefer a more chewy muesli cereal make a jar of *Ready-to-Eat Muesli**, and the family can help themselves. Similar made-up muesli mixtures can be bought from some health food shops who prepare their own, but avoid supermarket packeted muesli as they contain sugar and other unwanted additives.

In the winter a serving of porridge, topped with milk and honey, and maybe fresh or dried fruit, makes a perfect nourishing and warming breakfast food. A helping of bran can also be beneficial at breakfast time if necessary. (See page 29)

## ALL FRUIT BREAKFAST

Because many fruits, particularly the more acid fruits such as oranges, grapefruit and plums, have to differing extents an inhibiting effect on the digestion of protein and starch foods (See page 38), they could be considered more beneficial when eaten on their own. An all fruit breakfast for a change is cleansing, healthy and a perfect way to eat fruits of all kinds with maximum benefit, but make sure that some whole cereal food such as wholemeal bread is eaten later in the day.

## READY-TO-EAT MUESLI

1½ lbs oat flakes, or use a mixture of flaked oats, wheat, barley and rye
8 oz wheatgerm
3 oz sunflower seeds
3 oz chopped mixed nuts — peanuts, cashews, hazelnuts, walnuts, almonds, brazil nuts

2 oz sesame seeds
8 oz dried fruit — raisins, sultanas, currants, chopped dates, dried apple rings, banana chips, and apricots are all good.

Mix all together, and keep in an airtight jar in a cool place. These quantities make a large amount from which individual portions can be taken. Serve with milk, a little honey or raw sugar to taste, if necessary, and top with fresh low-acid fruits in season. A little bran or a bran cereal can be added as well if required.

Essentially a chewy cereal, *Ready-to-Eat Muesli\** can be put through a food grinder if you like: it's easier to eat and probably more digestible when ground, and young children will prefer it this way.

## WHEATGERM AND NUT MIX

8 oz wheatgerm
4 oz mixed nuts, finely
ground — peanuts,
almonds, hazelnuts and
walnuts

4 oz sunflower seeds, finely
ground
4 oz raisins

Mix all together and keep in an airtight jar to use as needed. Store in a cool place. This is a delicious high protein breakfast cereal mixture. Use in *Swiss Muesli*\*. Serve individual portions on its own with milk and honey, or sprinkle over any breakfast cereal to give it a tasty and healthy boost.

## SWISS MUESLI

**For 4**
3 oz oatmeal or rolled oats,
soaked overnight in 9
tablespoons water
Juice of ½ lemon
2 apples (unpeeled)
1-2 tablespoons honey

2 heaped tablespoons *Wheat-germ and Nut Mix*\*
6 tablespoons (or 1 carton)
of yoghurt (or use milk
or thin cream)

Just before serving, add lemon juice to soaked oats, and then grate the apples straight into the mixture so that the shavings do not brown. Add honey *Wheatgerm and Nut Mix*\* and yoghurt, and stir well.
If muesli is not to be eaten at once, keep airtight in the fridge.
A valuable breakfast food full of protein, vitamins and minerals; a perfect, healthy start to the day.

*Variation*
Replace all or some of the apples with chopped banana. Alternatively, prunes, apricots or other dried fruits that have been covered in boiling water and soaked overnight (but not cooked) can be chopped and added to the muesli.

## BRAN, FRUIT AND NUT CEREAL

**For 4**

2 oz dried apple rings
2 oz peanuts
2 oz sunflower seeds

2 oz 'Bran Buds' or 'All Bran'
2 oz wheatgerm
2 oz sultanas

Grind peanuts and sunflower seeds in a food grinder, chop apple rings, then mix with all other ingredients.

Serve with milk and honey and, if you like, top with sliced banana, fresh strawberries or other fruits in season.

---

## MIXED GRAIN PORRIDGE

**Grain Mix**

About 4 oz each of cracked wheat, flaked oats (jumbo

oats), barley, rye, wheat, brown rice

Mix the cereal flakes together and keep in an airtight jar to use as needed.

**To make porridge for 4**

Stir 2 cups of 'Grain Mix' into a pan with 4 cups of water and/or milk. Add 1 level teaspoon sea salt and leave to soak overnight. In the morning bring to the boil and, stirring frequently, simmer very gently for about 10 minutes until the porridge is thick. A little more milk could be added if it looks too thick for taste.

Serve with milk or yoghurt, raisins if you like, and honey to sweeten. Porridge can of course, be made in the same way from any of the above grains individually.

*Variation*
## Thermos Cooked Porridge

If you have a thermos flask or two (depending on their size), this is a marvellous method of cooking porridge overnight. Wide necked flasks are ideal as it is easier to get the cooked porridge out of these! And in the morning the porridge is hot and ready to eat with little more effort needed.

Measure out the cereal, water and milk, and salt as above, but bring the mixture to the boil, stirring. Remove from the heat and pour into the flask(s). In the morning reheat briefly in a pan, stirring in a little more milk to thin if necessary.

---

## QUICK PORRIDGE

**For 4**

Stir 2 cups of rolled oats into a pan with 4-5 cups of water or use a milk and water mixture. Add 1 level teaspoon salt. Bring to the boil stirring and simmer for 4 minutes.

*Variation*
## Extra Value Porridge

Add a handful each of raisins and chopped nuts to the milk and cook with the oats as before. Grated apple can be added just before serving or chopped dried apple cooked with the other ingredients.

Serve either porridge with milk, cream or yoghurt, and honey or raw cane sugar to taste.

---

## FRUIT BREAKFAST FOR ONE

In a bowl place a selection of dried fruit according to taste such as prunes, apple rings and apricots. Cover with boiling water and stir in a little honey and molasses. Leave fruit soaking overnight.

Next morning, the fruit can be topped with sliced banana or other fruits before eating. Accompany with a glass of fresh fruit juice.

*A lovely refreshing breakfast.*

---

## CRUNCHY TOASTED CEREAL

4 oz "Grain Mix" (see
*Mixed Grain Porridge**)
1 oz desiccated coconut
2 oz wheatgerm
2 oz mixed sunflower seeds,
almonds, peanuts and
hazelnuts, all chopped
finely
3 tablespoons honey
1 tablespoon vegetable oil
2 oz raisins

Combine the grain, coconut, wheatgerm and chopped nuts in a basin. Mix the honey and oil, pour onto the nuts and grains and mix well. Spread loosely onto a large greased baking tray and bake at No.3, 325°F, for 20-30 minutes, turning over with a wooden spoon two or three times during baking.
Remove when lightly golden. Cool, then mix with the raisins. Store in an airtight jar. Serve with milk as a breakfast cereal, eat dry as a snack or sprinkle onto puddings.

## FRUIT AND YOGHURT BREAKFAST

For 1 generous serving of a complete breakfast:
1 carton yoghurt
1 small banana, mashed
1 small eating apple, grated
1 dessertspoon each of bran,
wheatgerm, raisins
1 teaspoon honey
Dash of lemon juice

½ teaspoon of molasses
½-1 teaspoon brewers yeast } Optional*

*Molasses and brewers yeast are both rather strongly flavoured and adding them must depend on personal taste. But they do give a wonderful nutritional boost to your breakfast!
Mix all the ingredients together. Serve immediately or keep airtight in the fridge and eat the same day.

# *Vegetables*

Vegetables, together with fruits, are our main source of vitamin C, and contain many other valuable vitamins and minerals. But these nutrients are very easily destroyed by light, air, water and heat and the longer vegetables are exposed to these elements through storage or cooking, the less goodness they contain; the greatest nutritional benefit is obtained from most vegetables when they are eaten fresh, after a minimum amount of handling or cooking, and raw whenever possible. So in order to enjoy all vegetables at their best, some careful choosing, storage, preparation and cooking rules must be followed.

## CHOOSING

Always try to buy seasonal fresh vegetables in daily quantities or, if you grow your own, pick only as much as you need for a day.

To be sure of getting the greatest amount of vitamins and minerals, choose only the darker-coloured vegetables, avoiding pale, bleached greens, salads and carrots.

Vegetables (and fruits) ideally should be organically grown; that means without the use of chemical sprays. But if these are not available, they can be washed before eating in a mixture of 1 part vinegar to 4 parts water to remove any chemical residue.

Although seasonal fresh vegetables are preferable, frozen vegetables retain most of their nutrient value if frozen quickly when fresh. However, canned vegetables should be avoided.

## STORAGE

Root vegetables will keep fresh for several days if kept in a cool dark place and wrapped in paper or ventilated plastic bags. But all other leafy green vegetables and salad greens must be eaten within 24 hours, after which time they have lost most of their nutrients. Keep these vegetables in airtight plastic bags in the fridge where they will remain fresh and crisp, and never wash or prepare any vegetables until ready to use.

## PREPARATION AND COOKING

Prepare salads and vegetables for cooking only in the quantity immediately required.

To ensure maximum nutritional value, never peel with a knife. Use a peeler or better still scrub and eat the skins of both vegetables and fruit whenever possible. Retain as many dark green outer leaves of leafy vegetables as you can.

Prepare vegetables quickly to avoid too much contact with light and air. On no account leave any vegetables soaking but wash quickly in cold water. Washed and prepared salad vegetables can be dried, covered or wrapped, and put in the fridge to crisp until served, but do not add dressing until just before serving.

Cook with the minimum amount of boiling water, in a pan with a tightly fitting lid until just tender. Cooked vegetables should still be crisp and crunchy. Preserve cooking liquid, which contains vitamins and minerals, for soups and stocks. Serve vegetables immediately. Never reheat cooked vegetables, but most can be added cold to salads, avoiding waste. Salt is a destroyer of nutrients, as is bicarbonate of soda, so neither should ever be cooked with vegetables. Salt can be added to taste afterwards, but although I have suggested the addition of a little sea salt to taste with most of the vegetables listed, use of salt should be strictly limited at all times.

Individual cooking times and methods are given under separate vegetable headings. The cooking times are for fresh vegetables. Frozen vegetables will need less cooking time, as freezing tenderizes. Directions on commercial packets can be followed.

**Sauté-Steam Method** Wash vegetables briefly in cold water. Drain quickly and place in a pan with a tightly fitting lid. Add a little vegetable oil and a dash of water, lightly toss vegetables and cover tightly with lid. Cook for only a few minutes, shaking pan frequently to prevent sticking and ensure distribution.

This method enables the vegetables to steam quickly in their own juices with minimum nutrient loss.

Season vegetables finally with sea salt and pepper and serve immediately.

**Quick Simmer Method** Bring a small amount of water in a pan to the boil. Add prepared vegetables. Return to the boil and cook quickly. Season and serve immediately.

**Sauté Method** Heat a little vegetable oil or margarine in a pan with a tightly fitting lid. Add prepared vegetables and replace lid. Sauté, shaking pan to prevent sticking, for only a few minutes. Add sea salt and black pepper finally and serve immediately.

It is a good idea not to cook green leafy vegetables, carrots or others that need minimal cooking until everyone is ready to eat and all the food is about to be served. This lessens the risk of nutrient loss from over-cooking or keeping warm!

**Asparagus**
Trim asparagus stalks and wash the spears. Tie the pieces into a bundle and place in a pan of boiling water with the heads free. Cook for 15-30 minutes until tender, and serve hot with a little sea salt, pepper and vegetable margarine. Asparagus spears are very good served in a *Cheese*\* or *White Sauce*\*.

**Aubergine**
Aubergine has a tendency to be bitter so, before cooking, slice or dice the flesh according to the recipe, sprinkle generously with salt, and leave for at least ½ hour. During this time the bitter juices will drain away from the skins and the aubergine can then be rinsed with cold water. The salting process also stops the aubergine from absorbing too much oil when sautéd. This is a delicious and rather exotic vegetable, well worth taking time to prepare properly so that it can be enjoyed at its best.

**Beetroot**
Scrub the skins but do not peel, and to cook, boil in water until tender which will take anything up to an hour. Beetroots can otherwise be baked in a moderate oven for about 1½ hours. Peel cooked beetroot while still hot and serve immediately, sliced, seasoned with a little sea salt and pepper and dotted with vegetable margarine. Alternatively, serve in a warm *Sweet Herbal Yoghurt Sauce*\*.

**Broad Beans**
Broad beans supply some protein. Remove from pods only when ready to use, then add plenty of dried or fresh mint and thyme, and *Quick Simmer* for 10-20 minutes until just tender. Season and serve dotted with vegetable margarine mixed with chopped fresh herbs, or in a *White** or *Cheese Sauce**. To vary, onion slices cooked with broad beans make a good combination.

**Broccoli**
A good source of vitamins A, B and C, 'new' broccoli is lovely raw in a green salad. Split the larger stalks down the centre into two or flour. To cook, *Sauté-Steam* for only 2-3 minutes. Broccoli should be dark green and still crisp when cooked. Season with a little sea salt and ground pepper before serving. Broccoli is both tasty and nutritious served in a *Cheese** or *White Sauce**.

**Brussels Sprouts**
High in vitamin C content, these miniature cabbages are lovely sliced and eaten raw in green salads. Trim and wash quickly in cold water. To cook, leave whole, but make a deep slit in the stalk of each sprout with a small sharp knife. This will lessen the cooking time needed. Then *Quick Simmer* for about 5 minutes until only just tender. Sprouts must be still green and crisp. Season before serving with a little sea salt and pepper.

**Cabbage** all types, including Kale, Greens and others
All cabbage greens have a high nutritive value, and finely grated or shredded raw cabbage is a crunchy and deliciously healthy vegetable to eat in salads. Grate, slice or shred very thinly with a sharp knife, retaining as many outer dark green leaves as possible. Wash quickly in cold water. To cook, *Sauté-Steam* for only 2-3 minutes. Cooked cabbage must still be crisp and green. Serve immediately seasoned with a little sea salt and ground black pepper. For an interesting flavour, a teaspoon of caraway seeds can be cooked with the cabbage.

## Carrots

Full of vitamin A and minerals, carrots are exceptionally good eaten raw; thinly sliced or grated in salads, or served with a dip. A most nourishing vegetable!

Wash and scrub carrots, or peel only if the skins are 'old', and remove the tops and bottoms. To cook, slice as thinly as possible lengthwise, and *Sauté-Steam* for only 2-3 minutes — they should still be crunchy when cooked. Add a little sea salt and ground black pepper finally, a knob of vegetable margarine if you like, and sprinkle with chopped parsley.

Carrots are unusual and very good served with either *Piquant Yoghurt Dressing** or *Yoghurt Sunflower Seed Sauce**. Heat and pour over the carrots before serving.

## Cauliflower

Cauliflower florettes are delicious eaten raw either sliced and added to salads, or eaten with a dip.

To cook, break or cut into small florettes, wash quickly in cold water and drain. *Quick Simmer* for 5-10 minutes depending on the size of the florettes, but until only just tender. Cauliflower should still be crisp and the stalks green. Serve immediately seasoned with a little sea salt and freshly ground black pepper. Cauliflower can be served in a sauce too, such as one of the *White** or *Yoghurt Sauces**. For a quick and nutritious vegetable dish, served covered in a good *Cheese Sauce**.

## Corn

To cook on the cob, remove husks and silk and *Quick Simmer* for 5-10 minutes or until kernels are tender. Salt can be added to the water when cooking corn. Serve with vegetable margarine and seasoning to taste.

## Courgettes

Wash, cut off stalks, and slice thinly without peeling. *Sauté* for 3-5 minutes, shaking pan to prevent sticking, then add a little sea salt and black pepper and serve immediately. Courgettes are also delicious served with a *Cheese** or *Yoghurt Sauce** spooned over them, and stuffed courgettes make an excellent main meal (see *Stuffed Vegetables**)

**Green Beans**
Wash and string if necessary. Leave thin French beans whole, and slice thicker runner beans. *Quick Simmer* with a generous amount of herbs for 5-10 minutes until just tender. Serve seasoned with a little sea salt and pepper and dotted with vegetable margarine.
For an unusual bean dish, cook an onion sliced into thin rings with the beans and serve both in a warmed *Yoghurt Sunflower-Seed Sauce**.
Left-over cooked beans are very good cold added to a green salad. Or by tossing them in *Yoghurt and Mayonnaise Dressing** and serving on lettuce leaves, you can make an excellent cooked bean salad.

**Leeks**
Cut off roots and tough outer leaves. Slice and rinse in cold water. *Sauté* for 3-5 minutes shaking pan to prevent sticking. Alternatively after trimming leeks, leave whole and *Quick Simmer* until tender. Finally, add a little sea salt and black pepper and serve immediately in a *White**, *Herb** or *Cheese Sauce**.

**Marrow**
Peel marrow, trim ends and slice in half lengthwise. With a spoon, hollow out the woody seeded centres of each half and discard, then thinly slice and *Sauté* in vegetable margarine until tender — about 5 minutes. Can be served in a *Cheese Sauce** or one of the *Yoghurt Sauces**.

59

**Mushrooms**

Containing some B vitamins, mushrooms are as tasty eaten raw in salads or with a dip as they are cooked and served as a side dish. It is best to choose the firm button mushrooms for eating raw — I prefer these anyway and for cooking — but all mushrooms must be firm and really fresh to be enjoyed at their best.

Wash in cold water and shake dry. Peel and trim stalks if necessary and either leave whole or slice thinly through stalk and head. To cook, *Sauté*, shaking pan for 3-5 minutes. A dash of Worcestershire or soya sauce added to the pan gives a lovely flavour. Season as necessary and serve immediately. Large mushroom caps can be filled with a savoury stuffing and served as an unusual and very tasty main meal.

**Onions**

Onions are a marvellous flavourful vegetable, full of minerals and vitamin C as well as some of the B vitamins. Like garlic, they have medicinal properties too, being good for coughs and colds, and for purifying the blood. Certainly cooking would be very dull without the versatile onion and the savoury recipes in this book make full use of them.

**Parsnips**

Parsnips are a delicious winter vegetable. Peel and roast in the oven in a little vegetable oil until tender, or slice thinly, *Sauté-Steam* and serve dotted with vegetable margarine, seasoned with a little sea salt and black pepper.

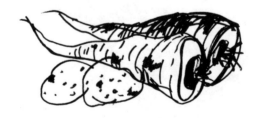

## Peas

Leave in the pods until ready to cook, then shell and add fresh or dried mint with 1 teaspoon brown sugar to the cooking water. *Quick Simmer* for 10-20 minutes until just tender. Served seasoned with a little sea salt and black pepper and dotted with vegetable margarine. This nourishing and popular vegetable is lovely served with *Sweet Herbal Yoghurt Sauce** or *Yoghurt Sunflower-Seed Sauce**.

## Potatoes

Potatoes are an incredibly versatile vegetable, and I think that most people have their own favourite methods of cooking and serving them. They retain most of their nutritive value when baked in their jackets. Scrub the skins under cold water, wrap in tinfoil and bake for approx 1 hour in a hot oven until tender; new potatoes are lovely cooked like this too.

To boil them, scrub the skins or peel them if they are tough, wash in cold water but never leave potatoes to soak, and *Quick Simmer* until tender. Fresh or dried mint added to the cooking water gives the potatoes a lovely fresh taste. Drain and serve with vegetable margarine dotted over the top, season and garnish with chopped parsley or mint. Boiled potatoes can be served in *Cheese Sauce** for a nutritious dish, or eaten cold with a salad meal. Mix with *Mayonnaise** or a *Yoghurt Dressing** for potato salad.

Alternatively, mash cooked potatoes with a little milk and vegetable margarine and season to taste. Reheat before serving or mix with grated cheese and beaten egg, then brown under the grill.

For an unusual potato dish, serve boiled potatoes, seasoned and hot, with a warmed *Yoghurt Sauce** poured over them, sprinkled with paprika. The variations are endless!

## Spinach

Spinach has a high vitamin and mineral content and should be eaten frequently. Leaves can be sliced or left whole in cooking, and young leaves can be finely shredded and added to a green salad. To cook, wash briefly in cold water and drain. *Sauté-Steam* for only 2-3 minutes so that spinach leaves are still crisp and green. Drain well, season with sea salt and pepper and serve. Alternatively top with a *White Sauce**.

Alternatively, put cooked spinach and its juice into a liquidizer, puree and season to taste before serving. Spinach puree is delicious thickened with some sour cream or, more economically, with a milk and flour mixture. In a cup, make a paste with a heaped teaspoon of flour and a little milk taken from about ¼ pint. Add the rest of the milk gradually and stir until smooth, then pour onto the spinach purée and stir over heat until thickened. Add a dash of lemon juice, some finely chopped parsley, and crushed garlic if you like. Serve immediately.

---

## STIR FRIED VEGETABLES

A marvellous way of cooking a selection of vegetables. Use any of the following, depending on the season, to produce a colourful and deliciously healthy vegetable side dish.
Prepare
**Onion** thinly sliced
**Garlic cloves** crushed
**Red or green peppers** seeded and sliced
**Carrots and parsnips** finely sliced lengthwise
**Celery sticks** sliced diagonally
**Cabbage or greens** shredded
**Leeks** trimmed, washed and sliced
**Button mushrooms** washed and sliced
**French beans** trimmed
**Courgettes** trimmed and sliced
**Cauliflower** broken into florettes

Lemon juice and fresh herbs as available (thyme, rosemary, parsley, mint) **OR** soya sauce

Heat 2-3 tablespoons vegetable oil in a large pan with a lid, and add any of the following: onion, garlic, peppers, carrots, parsnips and celery. Fry quickly stirring, then add any of the other vegetables mentioned above, a dash of boiling water (the steam from this will help cook the vegetables quickly) and 1 or 2 tablespoons lemon juice with some chopped fresh herbs. Or for an Eastern flavour, add 1 or 2 tablespoons soya sauce at this stage instead of lemon juice and herbs. Clamp the lid on the pan, lower heat slightly, and *Sauté-Steam* for a minute or two, shaking the pan frequently to distribute vegetables and prevent sticking. Serve immediately.

## HUNGARIAN MARROW

About 1 lb vegetable marrow
1-2 tablespoons vegetable oil
1 level tablespoon paprika

1 carton sour cream or
yoghurt

Peel marrow, cut in half lengthwise and scoop out centres with a spoon and discard. Slice very thinly, and *Sauté* in a mixture of the vegetable oil and paprika. Stir well and cook for 5-10 minutes until tender. Just before serving, thicken with sour cream or yoghurt and heat through without bringing to the boil.

## SWEET RED CABBAGE

About 1 lb red cabbage,
  finely shredded and with
  any thick stalk removed
2 oz vegetable margarine
2 apples, peeled and sliced

1 onion, finely shredded
1-2 tablespoons honey
Juice of 1 lemon
$\frac{1}{4}$ pint red wine
Sea salt and pepper

Melt the margarine in a large lidded pan and add the shredded cabbage and onion. Brown over a low heat stirring constantly. Add the remaining ingredients, cover the pan, and simmer for $1\frac{1}{2}$-2 hours, stirring occasionally. Season to taste before serving.

# *Salads and Appetizers*

One meal a day ought to be a salad meal containing plenty of fresh raw vegetables and fruits combined to make exciting and flavourful salads so that this meal need never be boring!

In the recipes for Protein Salads, protein is provided as well so that they are complete salad meals — perfect for slimmers. Or, served in smaller quantities as a first course, these salads will provide extra nourishment to a meal if necessary.

Salads make perfect starters because raw vegetables and fruit get the gastric juices flowing and are full of digestive enzymes to help in the digestion of protein. The Side Salads are ideal for serving before a meal, or they can replace cooked vegetables with a hot meal. Alternatively, accompany any of the Side Salads with protein in the form of a good cheese, a Protein Spread or Salad Dressing from the recipe section on page 80. Serve with fresh wholemeal bread or crispbread, and you have a delicious salad meal.

## PROTEIN SALADS

### COLESLAW

½ lb finely shredded cabbage — any type of white or red
2 carrots, grated
1 small onion, finely sliced or 6 spring onions, chopped (onions could be left out of the slaw, especially if for children)

1 eating apple, grated or finely sliced, and tossed in lemon juice
2 sticks of celery, finely sliced
1 teaspoon caraway seeds (optional)

½ quantity of *Yoghurt and Mayonnaise Dressing**

Mix vegetables well. Add dressing and combine.

*Variations*
Add chopped fresh orange or pineapple to the slaw. Or for a more substantial fruit and nut version add 2oz chopped nuts or sunflower seeds, and dried fruit such as sultanas, chopped dried apricots or dates.

### CAULIFLOWER, CARROT AND APPLE

1 small head of cauliflower, grated or finely chopped
2-4 new carrots, grated
1 eating apple, chopped small or grated

Dressing: *French Dressing** or lemon juice

A bunch of spring onions
1 green pepper, thinly sliced (optional)
2 tablespoons raisins
2 tablespoons toasted peanuts
*Yoghurt and Tahina** to serve separately

Mix all salad ingredients and toss in a little *French Dressing** or lemon juice. Pile on lettuce leaves. Serve with an accompanying bowl of *Yoghurt and Tahina**: this provides complete protein from the combined peanuts, sesame and yoghurt. It tastes good too!

## YOGHURT AND CUCUMBER

1 cucumber, peeled and very
  finely sliced
⅓ pint approx yoghurt

1 tablespoon finely chopped
  mint
Sea salt and black pepper

Sprinkle cucumber slices generously with salt and leave for about 30 minutes. Drain off liquid, rinse through a colander, and squeeze out well. Mix with yoghurt, mint and seasoning.

*A wonderfully refreshing salad containing protein. Excellent with curry.*

## FRUIT SALAD WITH COTTAGE CHEESE DRESSING

Mix together a selection of chopped fruits such as apples, pears, bananas, melon, peaches, grapes, pineapple, oranges, seasonal fruits and berries. Pile onto individual lettuce lined plates, top with *Cottage Cheese Dressing*\*, sprinkle with chopped nuts or sunflower seeds and maybe some crystallized ginger.
*A delicious and healthy protein salad meal.*

## AVOCADO AND MELON

Mix together equal quantities of chopped avocado (tossed in lemon juice) and melon. Serve in scooped out avocado shells topped with yoghurt as a refreshing starter or a super low-calorie protein salad. Instead of plain yoghurt, *Sweet Herbal Yoghurt Dressing*\* or *Yoghurt and Mayonnaise Dressing*\* could be used.

For a more substantial meal, this salad is lovely with added sliced banana, and topped with *Cottage Cheese Dressing*\*. Garnish with sunflower seeds.

## WALDORF SALAD

2 eating apples, diced
4-6 sticks celery, sliced
4 tablespoons yoghurt, or
  ½ quantity *Yoghurt and*
  *Mayonnaise Dressing*\*

2oz chopped mixed nuts
2oz raisins or chopped dates


Mix all ingredients together.
*A lovely protein salad.*

## CABBAGE, APPLE AND PEANUT SALAD

About ½ lb finely grated
  cabbage
2 grated eating apples

4 oz roasted peanuts
1 tablespoon *Mayonnaise**

Mix all ingredients together.
*A quick salad that is a favourite with most children.*

## AVOCADOS WITH COTTAGE CHEESE DRESSING

2 avocado pears, halved and
  stoned
Lettuce leaves

*Cottage Cheese Dressing**
  mixed with
1 tablespoon sunflower seeds
  or chopped nuts

Pile dressing into avocado halves and serve on lettuce leaves.

Avocado halves served in this way make super appetizers or protein salads, serve as a complete salad meal, fill avocados with a larger amount of *Cottage Cheese Dressing**.

*Variation*
Avocados are also good filled with *Curd and Blue Cheese Dip**.

## PEARS WITH COTTAGE CHEESE

2 pears, halved and cored
Lemon juice
*Cottage Cheese Dressing**
2 tablespoons sunflower seeds
  or chopped nuts

Some chopped crystallized
  ginger (optional)
Grapes or strawberries to
  decorate

Brush surfaces of pears with lemon juice. Mix sunflower seeds or nuts and ginger (if using) with *Cottage Cheese Dressing**. Pile mixture onto pears. Serve on lettuce leaves decorated with grapes or strawberries. Slices of pineapple or tiny melon halves can be served in the same way, and all make refreshing protein salads or appetizers.

Quantities given serve 4 as an appetizer or 2 as a protein salad meal.

*Variation*
Use *Creamy Peanut Butter Spread** to fill fruit.

## SALAD NICOISE

Lettuce

French beans, lightly cooked
then chilled

Potatoes, cooked then chilled
(optional)

Tomatoes, cut into wedges

Hard boiled eggs

Olives

Capers

Spring onions, or onion rings

Green pepper cut into thin
slices

*French Dressing**

On a bed of whole or shredded lettuce leaves, place beans, potatoes (if using), onions, peppers and tomatoes. Top with hard boiled egg cut into halves or quarters, and garnish with olives and capers. Trickle *French Dressing** over the top before serving.

*An unusual, sustaining and very tasty protein salad.*

## STUFFED EGGS

4 hard boiled eggs

Pinch of dry mustard

2 teaspoons *French Dressing**

8 oz cottage cheese

Sea salt and black pepper

$\frac{1}{2}$ teaspoon paprika

1 teaspoon chopped chives or
spring onions

Fresh parsley and olives
to garnish

Cut the eggs in halves lengthwise and remove the yolks. Mash the yolks with other ingredients and fill the egg whites with the mixture. Arrange the stuffed eggs on a bed of shredded lettuce and garnish with sprigs of fresh parsley and olive slices.

## AUBERGINE AND YOGHURT SALAD

2-3 aubergines, peeled and
  very thinly sliced
1-2 cloves garlic, finely
  chopped

½ pint yoghurt
Chopped fresh parsley and
  paprika to garnish

Sprinkle aubergine slices lightly with salt and leave for about ½ hour. Rinse thoroughly with cold water, then squeeze out. Place slices in a greased shallow oven dish and dot with garlic. Cover with tinfoil and bake in a moderate oven until tender — about 1 hour. Then mash with a fork and leave to cool. Mix with yoghurt, spoon into a serving dish, chill and serve sprinkled with paprika and chopped parsley.

*Variation*
Add 6 skinned and chopped tomatoes to salad.

## BEETROOT AND YOGHURT SALAD

1 lb beetroot, boiled and
  chopped
½ pint yoghurt

Chopped parsley and onion
  rings to garnish

*Dressing:*  1 tablespoon olive
              oil
            1 tablespoon apple
              cider vinegar

1 tablespoon honey
Sea salt and
  pepper

Toss beetroot in mixed dressing ingredients, then combine with the yoghurt and pile into a serving bowl. Serve chilled, garnished with chopped parsley and onion rings.

---

## RICE SALAD

8 oz brown rice, cooked until tender in 1¼ pints salted boiling water (see method on page 116) and cooled after cooking

½ lb packet frozen mixed vegetables, cooked lightly and chilled

2-4 tablespoons *French Dressing**

1 green or red pepper, seeded and finely chopped or sliced

1 onion or large bunch of spring onions, finely chopped

4 oz button mushrooms, wiped and thinly sliced

4 oz roasted nuts — peanuts, cashews or almonds

2 tomatoes, chopped

Bunch of parsley, finely chopped

Chopped fresh herbs, as available

Sea salt and black pepper

Hard boiled eggs to decorate

Mix ingredients together, and serve chilled, piled onto a platter and decorated with wedges of hard boiled egg.

*A lovely summer protein salad.*

---

## SIDE SALADS

**Tossed Green Salad**
The most attractive of salads, this can be also the simplest, consisting of only shredded cold crisp lettuce leaves and maybe some spring onions. Toss lightly in a good *French Dressing** and you have a delightful side salad. But by combining a wider variety of raw salad greens and herbs, a greater range of nutrients is contained in the salad, and the result looks, tastes and is deliciously healthy!

Wash all greens well a little in advance to allow time for drying and crisping. Shake excess water gently from them, wrap lightly in plastic bags and put in the fridge to chill and crisp. Prepare salad greens by tearing them or slicing lightly with a very sharp knife. Too much handling of green leaves bruises them and destroys vitamin C. Be sure to use as many dark green outer leaves as possible as these contain more nutrients.

*Combine a mixture of any of the following*

Lettuce
Cabbage, spinach, broccoli or kale leaves
Brussels sprouts, shredded
Cucumber
Celery and young celery leaves
Spring onions
Onion rings
Green peppers, seeded and finely sliced
Cauliflower florettes
Chicory
Chinese leaves
Watercress
Mustard cress
Bean sprouts
Young dandelion leaves
Young parsnip, carrot or turnip tops, in small quantities
Fresh parsley and mint
Any other fresh herbs according to taste — try chives, fennel, rosemary, thyme basil, marjoram and sage
*French Dressing**

Slice or tear all to required size, but wrap in polythene and keep in the fridge until ready to eat. Transfer to a salad bowl and toss in *French Dressing** just before serving.

---

## CUCUMBER AND TOMATO SALAD

1 cucumber
4 tomatoes, or more

Parsley
*French Dressing**

Peel and very thinly slice cucumber, then sprinkle slices generously with sea salt and leave for about 30 minutes. Drain liquid, rinse with cold water, then squeeze out well. Cut tomatoes into wedges. Arrange cucumber and tomato wedges in a salad bowl, trickle with *French Dressing** and sprinkle with chopped parsley.

---

## GREEK SALAD

1 lettuce, crisp, cold and
   shredded
1 green pepper, seeded and
   finely sliced
1 onion, cut into thin rings
4 tomatoes, cut into quarters
Green or black olives as
   as required

Fresh parsley, chopped
Fresh mint, chopped
Other herbs to add could
   include: fresh rosemary,
   dill, oregano, basil and
   chives

*Dressing:* juice of ½-1 lemon
      1 tablespoon
        olive oil
      sea salt and black
        pepper

Alternatively use
1-2 tablespoons of
   *French Dressing**

Mix salad ingredients, except tomatoes. Wrap in polythene and keep in the fridge until needed. Then place in a salad bowl, top with tomatoes and trickle over the combined dressing ingredients or *French Dressing** just before serving. Serve with slices of Feta cheese (a hard white salty goats' cheese, available from most good delicatessens) or another type of cheese.

## CARROT, CELERY AND RAISIN SALAD

4-6 large new carrots, grated
4 sticks celery, finely chopped
Handful of raisins

Grated orange peel (so rich in
   vitamin C)
Juice of 1 orange

Mix ingredients. Place in a lettuce lined salad bowl and garnish with fresh parsley and onion rings.

## CARROT VINAIGRETTE

4-6 carrots, finely grated
A bunch of spring onions,
  finely chopped

Parsley
Lettuce
*French Dressing**

Mix grated carrots and onions. Pile onto lettuce leaves, trickle fairly generously with *French Dressing**, and garnish with sprigs of parsley.

## CARROT AND GREEN SALAD

4 carrots, grated
1 orange, finely chopped
Large bunch of any or a
   mixture of finely chopped
   watercress, dandelion
   leaves, parsley, mustard
   and cress

1 small onion sliced into
   rings to garnish
Roasted chopped nuts
   (optional)

Mix salad ingredients. Pile onto a lettuce lined plate and garnish with onion rings, and nuts if using. *French Dressing** can be trickled over the top.

*A super tonic salad which has a cleansing effect upon the whole system.*

## RAW ROOT SALAD

Fresh new carrots
   swedes, parsnips
   or turnips
   beetroot
   radishes
   (all of these raw)

Orange peel
Cress or parsley to garnish

Wash and scrub vegetables but do not peel if possible. Grate individually all except radishes, mixing a little orange peel with the swedes, parsnips or turnips. Arrange the grated vegetables in individual piles, side by side, around a plate. Place radishes in the middle and garnish with cress or parsley. Serve with a bowl of *Yoghurt and Mayonnaise Dressing** or *Sweet Herbal Yoghurt Dressing**.

*This is a very unusual and highly decorative salad.*

## MUSHROOM AND TOMATO SALAD

½ lb button mushrooms,
  washed and sliced
4 tomatoes, cut into fine
  wedges
1 onion, cut into rings

1 green or red pepper,
  seeded and finely sliced
Fresh mint and parsley,
  chopped
*French Dressing**

Combine vegetables and mix well with 1-2 tablespoons of *French Dressing**.

## MUSHROOM AND PEPPER SALAD

1 green pepper, thinly sliced
1 red pepper, thinly sliced

4 oz button mushrooms,
  thinly sliced
8 black olives

Mix all ingredients together and serve with an accompanying bowl of *Yoghurt and Mayonnaise Dressing** or *Sweet Herbal Yoghurt Dressing**.

## BEETROOT AND APPLE SALAD

4 medium sized beetroot,
  peeled
2 eating apples

2 tablespoons *French
  Dressing**

Coarsely grate beetroot and unpeeled apples. Add dressing and mix well together. Serve on a bed of lettuce and garnish with onion rings.

## TOMATO SALAD

Tomatoes as many as required, cut into wedges

Onion rings, or chopped spring onions

Fresh mint or parsley, chopped

*French Dressing** (optional)

Sea salt and ground black pepper

Combine tomatoes, onions and herbs, season with salt and pepper. Top with *French Dressing**, if using.

*Full of all the goodness tomatoes contain, an easy and excellent salad. A perfect accompaniment to a quick ploughman's lunch (with wholemeal bread of course!)*

## GREEN SPLIT PEA SALAD

8 oz green split peas, soaked overnight or for a few hours

1 teaspoon sea salt

1 onion, finely chopped

2 tablespoons finely chopped parsley

1 tablespoon finely chopped mint

Drain soaked split peas and cover with fresh water. Add salt and bring to the boil. Cook for 30-50 minutes until tender. Drain well. While still warm, stir in finely chopped onion, parsley, mint and mixed dressing ingredients. Check seasoning, and place in a dish. Serve chilled, garnished with slices of tomato or twists of lemon.

*Variation*

A *Brown Lentil Salad* can be made by the same method but after soaking these will need more cooking time; about $3/4$-$1\frac{1}{2}$ hours. Then proceed as for *Green Split Pea Salad** but omit the mint and add $\frac{1}{2}$ teaspoon ground cumin or coriander instead. Garnish with wedges of hard boiled egg.

## SAVOURY FRENCH ROLL

Make this the day before it is needed. A wonderful picnic salad, which needs only to be accompanied with, for example, cheese to provide protein.

1 large wholemeal French
   loaf
1 green and 1 red pepper,
   seeded and cored
1½ oz black olives, stoned
2 oz green olives, stoned
1½ oz gherkins
1½ oz capers
2 sticks celery

4 tomatoes
1 small onion, or a bunch of
   spring onions
Fresh mint
Olive oil to bind if
   necessary
Pinch paprika, sea salt and
   pepper

Finely chop peppers, olives, gherkins, capers, celery, tomatoes, onions and mint. Mix well.

Cut the loaf lengthwise and remove the insides. Add these breadcrumbs to the vegetable mixture. Season well with paprika, salt and pepper, and moisten with olive oil if the mixture looks too dry.

Fill the halves of the loaf with the mixture. Put together, wrap in foil, and if possible leave for 24 hours in the fridge.

To serve, cut into thick slices.

## CHILLED STUFFED VINE LEAVES

If not lucky enough to have a supply of fresh vine leaves available, you can usually buy tinned or preserved vine leaves in most good delicatessens or Middle Eastern food shops.

About 2 dozen large vine
   leaves, or 4 oz in weight
4 oz brown rice
1 tomato, skinned and
   mashed
1 small onion or 1 bunch of
   spring onions, finely
   chopped

1 tablespoon finely chopped
   parsley
1 tablespoon finely chopped
   mint
1 clove garlic, crushed
½ teaspoon dill
Sea salt and black pepper
Pinch of mixed spice or
   coriander

*Dressing:* 2 tablespoons    Juice of ½ lemon    Sea salt and
vegetable oil    1 teaspoon honey    pepper

Cook rice in about ¾ pint boiling water until tender (see page 116), then mix well with all other stuffing ingredients. Soften the vine leaves in boiling salted water for a few minutes or, if using tinned or preserved leaves, rinse well in cold water.

Put about 1 teaspoon of stuffing mixture on the veined side of each leaf. Fold the sides of the leaves into the middle and then roll up. Place securely side by side in a greased overproof dish. Mix dressing ingredients and pour over the leaves. Cover with foil, and bake at No.4, 350°F for about ½-¾ hour. Cool in the dish, then remove and chill before serving.

Serve on a bed of lettuce or fresh vine leaves, and garnish with slices of lemon.

*These Middle Eastern delicacies make an unusual and delicious appetizer or side salad.*

## TABBOULEH

A delicious cracked wheat salad from the Middle East.

½ lb fine bulgar (cracked wheat)    3 tablespoons finely chopped fresh mint
3 tablespoons finely chopped spring onions    4 tablespoons olive oil
1 large onion, very finely chopped    4 tablespoons lemon juice or more
Sea salt and black pepper    Cooked, chilled vine leaves or raw lettuce leaves to serve
1 cup finely chopped parsley

Soak bulgar in water for about ½ hour before preparing salad. It will swell a lot. Drain, squeeze out and spread on a clean cloth if possible to dry further.

Mix the bulgar with all other ingredients and mix well. Taste, adjust seasoning as required, and add more lemon juice if necessary — tabbouleh should have a fresh lemony taste.

Serve on individual leaf lined plates or pile up on a large serving dish and decorate with olives, tomato quarters and sprigs of parsley.

*Traditionally, this salad is eaten with vine leaves with which to scoop up the salad. It makes a lovely party dish, appetizer or side salad.*

## TOMATO MOULD

6 teaspoons (or 1½ envelopes) gelatine
4 tablespoons hot water
½ pint tomato juice
1 lb tomatoes, skinned and chopped
Fresh mint, parsley or basil to taste

1 tablespoon apple cider vinegar or lemon juice
2 tablespoons tomato purée
1 teaspoon honey
Sea salt and pepper

Dissolve gelatine in hot water, then blend with all other ingredients, either in a blender or with a food mixer. Pour into a 1½ pint mould, and chill in the fridge until set.

Turn out and garnish with cress or parsley.

## MUSHROOMS À LA GRECQUE

1 onion, very thinly sliced
2 cloves garlic, crushed
2 tablespoons olive oil
¼ pint dry white wine
1 lb button mushrooms

½ lb tomatoes, skinned and chopped
1 teaspoon mixed herbs
Chopped parsley to garnish

Sauté onions and garlic in oil until tender. Add other ingredients and cook gently for 10 minutes.

Serve chilled as a starter, sprinkled with parsley.

## SPREADS, PÂTÉS, DIPS AND DRESSINGS

Nutritious spreads, pâtés and dips are as ideal for parties, snacks and appetizers as they are for protein providers in a salad meal. An attractive and healthy salad snack or start to any meal is a platter of crisp raw vegetables served with a refreshing dip. Try cauliflower florettes, carrots, spring onions, tomatoes, celery, mushrooms, and experiment with others. But be sure all the vegetables are crisp, cold and fresh!

As well as the classic salad dressings — *French Dressing** and *Mayonnaise** — I have included a selection of dressings made from yoghurt and cottage cheese. These are delightful protein boosters for a salad and, because they contain no oil, are better for the figure! Some of them also double up as dips.

## HUMMUS

This excellent Middle Eastern salad is high in the complete protein of chick peas and sesame combined, and is delicious served with a green salad and wholemeal bread or crispbread, or as a dip for raw vegetables. An ideal appetizer, party dish, or protein filled addition to a salad meal.

4 oz chick peas — soaked overnight in plenty of cold water
Juice of 2 lemons
2 tablespoons olive oil
¼ pint Tahina (sesame seed paste bought from health food shops or delicatessens)
1 teaspoon paprika
1 tablespoon chopped mint and/or parsley
2 cloves garlic — crushed
Sea salt to taste

Boil the chick peas in the same water that they were soaked in with some added salt, for about 2 hours or until tender. Drain, conserving water, and purée them in a liquidizer or blender along with the oil, lemon juice and enough of the cooking water to make it easy to blend. If a blender is not available, mash the chick peas thoroughly and mix with all other ingredients afterwards. Then add Tahina, garlic, paprika and herbs and mix to form a creamy paste. Add more of the liquid if necessary, and season with sea salt to taste.

## CURD CHEESE

A high protein, low calorie, creamy cheese can easily be made from yoghurt, and, as it is a perfect base for so many dips, spreads and other recipes, it is well worth making regularly.

Place yoghurt in a clean muslin or fine cotton cloth and tie the ends together. Hang over the kitchen tap and allow the yoghurt to drip for several hours or ideally overnight. Season with a little salt and pepper if you like. Paprika, grated onion, garlic or pepper, and chopped fresh herbs all add delightful flavours.

## CURRIED CURD CHEESE DIP

8 oz *Curd Cheese**
¼ pint yoghurt (or less)
1 teaspoon honey
2 teaspoons *Mayonnaise**

1 teaspoon curry powder OR
1 teaspoon garam masala
for a more gentle flavour
½ teaspoon turmeric

Blend ingredients together thoroughly, adding enough yoghurt to make a creamy dip. This will depend on the texture of the curd cheese.

## TANDOORI DIP

As above, but use 1 teaspoon tandoori powder instead of curry powder and omit turmeric.

## LIPTAUER CHEESE

The recipe for this popular Hungarian cheese spread should include ½ teaspoon anchovy paste, but for confirmed vegetarians it tastes equally good without.

8 oz *Curd Cheese*\*
2 oz vegetable margarine
1 tablespoon finely chopped
  onion, spring onions or
  fresh chives

½ teaspoon caraway seeds
½ teaspoon capers, chopped
1 teaspoon paprika
½ teaspoon sea salt
Black pepper

Mix all the ingredients well together with an electric beater or wooden spoon. Transfer to a suitable dish, cover in foil and chill in the fridge for several hours or overnight. Serve with wholemeal toast or crispbread.

## CURD AND BLUE CHEESE DIP

8 oz *Curd Cheese*\*
2-4 oz blue cheese, crumbled
¼-½ pint yoghurt — quantity
  will depend on how much

blue cheese is used and on
the texture of the curd
cheese.

Blend all ingredients together, adding enough yoghurt to make a smooth creamy dip.

## AVOCADO AND CHEESE PÂTÉ

2 avocados
8 oz *Curd Cheese*\* or cottage
  cheese
1 tablespoon yoghurt (or use
  *Mayonnaise*\* or cream)

1 tablespoon finely chopped
  spring onions or chives
½ teaspoon paprika
Sea salt and pepper to taste
Parsley to garnish
Dash of tabasco (optional)

Cut the avocado pears in half, remove stones and scoop out the flesh. Mash or blend flesh with other ingredients to a smooth consistency. Spoon into small individual dishes, garnish with parsley and maybe slices of hard boiled egg.

*A delicately flavoured refreshing appetizer, which can also be served as a raw vegetable dip.*

## YOGHURT AND TAHINA

¼ pint yoghurt
¼ pint Tahina (sesame seed paste)
2 cloves garlic, crushed
Juice of ½-1 lemon to taste

Sea salt to taste
1 tablespoon finely chopped parsley
½ teaspoon paprika

Mix ingredients together with whisk or mixer, seasoning to taste with lemon juice and salt.

Serve as a dip for raw vegetables or as a salad dressing.

Garnish with roasted nuts or chopped hard boiled egg, and eat with fresh wholemeal bread and a side salad for a protein salad meal.

## CREAMY PEANUT BUTTER SPREAD

A favourite with most children and filled with lots of energy-giving protein. Spread it generously onto slices of wholemeal toast for a perfect children's breakfast or tea. Try serving slices of banana on top!

8 oz cottage cheese
2 tablespoons yoghurt

1-2 teaspoons honey (optional)
2 tablespoons peanut butter

Mix ingredients together and beat or blend until smooth. For an excellent 'grown up' pâté, omit honey and add a dash of tabasco and maybe some chopped fresh herbs. Season to taste with salt and pepper.

## CURD CHEESE SPREAD
## WITH PINEAPPLE AND NUTS

8 oz *Curd Cheese** or cottage cheese
2 tablespoons yoghurt
4 slices of tinned pineapple, finely chopped (buy the unsweetened variety)
2 tablespoons nuts or seeds. Use: sunflower seeds,

roasted hazelnuts (chopped), toasted sesame seeds, flaked almonds, or try coconut and add 1 teaspoon of honey too.
Some finely chopped crystallized ginger (optional)

Mix ingredients well together.

## EGG AND COTTAGE CHEESE

8 oz cottage cheese
2 hard boiled eggs
1 tablespoon yoghurt
1 tablespoon finely chopped
 spring onions or chives

½ teaspoon poppy seeds or
 caraway seeds
2 teaspoons *French Dressing**
¼ teaspoon dry mustard
1 teaspoon paprika
Sea salt to taste

Mix ingredients together in a blender or mash well to combine.
*A high protein, low calorie dip or spread.*

## QUICK EGG AND CHEESE SANDWICH FILLING

4 oz cottage cheese
1 hard boiled egg
1 teaspoon *Mayonnaise**

Pinch paprika, sea salt and
 pepper

Mash all together to mix.

## GUACAMOLE (AVOCADO APPETIZER)

Flesh of 2 ripe avocados
Juice of 1 lemon
1 clove of garlic, finely
 chopped or grated
½ green pepper, finely
 chopped

1 tablespoon chopped fresh
 parsley, if available
1-2 tablespoons olive oil
Sea salt and black pepper
1 teaspoon paprika
Dash of tabasco (optional)

Mash avocados into lemon juice and then add all other ingredients.
Stir well. Alternatively, place all ingredients into a food blender,
and blend until smooth.

Guacamole is best served immediately, but if this is not possible,
place the avocado stones into the sauce until ready to serve. This
will help to keep the avocado from going brown for a little while.
Serve with fresh wholemeal bread, unleavened bread or garlic
bread.

*Guacamole can also be served as a vegetable dip.*

## FRENCH DRESSING (VINAIGRETTE)

3 tablespoons lemon juice, apple cider vinegar or wine vinegar
3 tablespoons olive oil
6 tablespoons vegetable oil
1 teaspoon sea salt and ground black pepper
1 clove garlic, crushed
1 teaspoon honey

1 teaspoon mustard powder
Herbs to taste — altogether about 2 tablespoons fresh or 1 tablespoon dried, taking any or a misture of herbs, such as: mint, parsley, thyme, rosemary, basil, oregano, chervil, chives, dill, tarragon

Put all ingredients in a screw-top jar and shake well to mix. The dressing can be kept in the fridge for an indefinite length of time, to be used when needed.

## MAYONNAISE

1 egg
8 fluid oz salad oil — I use half olive oil and half vegetable oil
1 teaspoon mustard powder

1 teaspoon honey
Sea salt and black pepper
1 tablespoon lemon juice or vinegar

Liquidize all ingredients except oil to mix well, then add the oil gradually through the lid while liquidizing; a drop at a time at first until the mixture begins to thicken, then more rapidly. The mayonnaise should be smooth and thick when finished and can then be kept in a jar in the fridge for a week or two.

## COTTAGE CHEESE DRESSING

8 oz *Curd Cheese\** or cottage cheese

2 tablespoons yoghurt or *Mayonnaise\** (or use a mixture)

1 tablespoon chopped spring onions, chives or parsley

½ teaspoon paprika

Sea salt and black pepper

Mix all ingredients together. Liquidize for a smoother salad dressing or vegetable dip.

*This dressing is excellent in avocado pear, and will fill 4 halves as an appetizer, or 2 halves for a protein salad meal.*

## YOGHURT AND MAYONNAISE DRESSING

4 tablespoons yoghurt

4 tablespoons *Mayonnaise\**

1 teaspoon honey

1 teaspoon paprika (optional)

Dash of tabasco (optional)

Sea salt

Mix ingredients well.

## CURRIED YOGHURT AND MAYONNAISE DRESSING

4 tablespoons yoghurt

4 tablespoons *Mayonnaise\**

1 teaspoon honey

1 teaspoon curry powder, garam masala or tandoori powder

Mix well together.

## SWEET HERBAL YOGHURT DRESSING OR SAUCE

½ pint yoghurt

1 teaspoon honey

1 tablespoon chopped fresh herbs as available: parsley,

basil, marjoram and spring onions are all good

1 teaspoon paprika

Mix all ingredients together and let stand for a while before serving.

*This dressing can also be warmed through and served as a sauce with cooked vegetables. Lovely with peas, courgettes, marrow, french beans, potatoes and beetroot.*

## PIQUANT YOGHURT DRESSING OR SAUCE

½ pint yoghurt
½ teaspoon turmeric
2 teaspoons lemon juice
Sea salt to taste

1 teaspoon each chopped
fresh mint and thyme,
rosemary or sage as
available

Mix ingredients and let stand for a while.

*Serve cold with salads or warm through without boiling and serve
with a curry dish or with vegetables such as cauliflower, vegetable
marrow, potato and carrots.*

# Sauces

## BASIC WHITE SAUCE

2 oz vegetable margarine
2 rounded tablespoons
  wholewheat flour
1 pint of milk, or ¾ pint
  milk and ¼ pint white wine

Sea salt and ground black
  pepper to taste
1 bay leaf

Melt margarine in a pan, then add flour and cook gently, stirring, until all the flour is frothy. Remove from heat, and stir in the milk or milk and wine, and the bay leaf. Return to heat, and stir until smooth and thick. Season with salt and pepper. Remove bay leaf before serving.

*Variations*

**Cheese Sauce**
Add 4-6 oz grated cheese to *White Sauce**

**Mushroom Sauce**
Add ½ lb finely chopped button mushrooms to *White Sauce** with a dash of Worcestershire sauce. Simmer for a few minutes to cook.

**Egg Sauce**
Add 2-3 chopped hard boiled eggs to *White Sauce**.

**Parsley Sauce**
Add 2 handfuls of finely chopped fresh parsley to *White Sauce**. Or add 2 tablespoons dried parsley and cook gently for a few minutes. Other herbs can be used instead of parsley to flavour sauce.

**Onion Sauce**
Sauté 1-2 finely chopped onions in the vegetable margarine before adding the flour, then proceed as for *White Sauce**.

---

## TOMATO SAUCE

2 tablespoons vegetable oil
1 onion, finely chopped or
  grated
1 clove garlic, crushed
2 level tablespoons
  wholewheat flour
1 pint water or vegetable
  stock

4 tablespoons tomato purée
$\frac{1}{2}$ teaspoon yeast extract
1 teaspoon honey
Sea salt and black pepper to
  taste
1-2 tablespoons sherry
  (optional)
pinch mixed herbs

Sauté the onion and garlic gently in the oil until tender, then add the flour and stir until frothy. Remove from the heat and stir in water or stock, return to heat and bring to the boil, stirring until thick. Add all other ingredients and simmer gently for 5 minutes.

---

## WINE SAUCE

2 tablespoons vegetable oil
1 onion, finely chopped or
grated
1 clove garlic, crushed
2 level tablespoons
wholeweat flour
½-¾ pint water or stock

Red or white wine to make
liquid up to 1 pint
1 tablespoon tomato purée
1 teaspoon honey
½ teaspoon yeast extract
Pinch of mixed herbs
Sea salt and pepper, to taste

Sauté the onion and garlic in the oil until soft. Add the flour and
stir until frothy, then remove from the heat and stir in water or
stock and wine. Return to heat and bring to the boil stirring all the
time until thickened. Add the remainder of the ingredients and
simmer gently for 5 minutes.

## ITALIAN TOMATO SAUCE

Excellent with spaghetti or other pasta dishes. See page 112

## AUBERGINE AND TOMATO SAUCE

A variation of the *Italian Tomato Sauce*\*. See page 113

## CURRY SAUCE

A good base for many quick curry meals. See page 120

## YOGHURT SUNFLOWER-SEED SAUCE

½ pint yoghurt
2oz finely ground sunflower
seeds

½ teaspoon paprika
Sea salt to taste

Mix ingredients. Warm through, stirring, but do not boil.
Serve poured over cauliflower, carrots, beans, peas or potatoes.

## YOGHURT SAUCES

**Sweet Herbal Yoghurt Sauce**   See page 86
**Piquant Yoghurt Sauce**   See page 87

# *Soups*

A good home-made vegetarian soup is an excellent start to any meal, and soups made from vegetables have the added bonus of being especially quick and easy to make. I have included here a small selection of my favourites, and there is always an abundance of alternative seasonal vegetables around which can be made up into other delicious soups by using the same methods. Learn to experiment; health food shops sell vegetable stock cubes to enhance the flavour of any soup, and although a liquidizer is a great asset, soup can be puréed quite successfully through a sieve or food mincer.

Substantial soups such as those containing dried peas and beans form tasty and nourishing meals in themselves, served with wholemeal bread to complete the protein content or maybe with *Cheese Straws** on page 168. Provide a side salad or fruit to follow. And in the summer, refreshing *Gazpacho** is perfect before a salad, full of vitamins, minerals and unbeatable Italian flavour.

## BRUSSELS SPROUT SOUP

1 lb Brussels sprouts, washed,
  and trimmed if necessary
2 large onions, roughly
  chopped
1 clove garlic, crushed

Yoghurt to serve
  (optional)

2 pints water
1 vegetable stock cube
1 tablespoon parsley
1 teaspoon each oregano and
  thyme

Sea salt and black pepper

Bring water to the boil, then add soup ingredients. Simmer for about 10-15 minutes (sprouts should be tender but still green, otherwise they tend to be bitter).

Liquidize the soup, then return to the pan, season to taste with salt and pepper, and serve.

About 1 tablespoon of warmed yoghurt is very good added to swirl around each individual bowl of Sprout Soup on serving.

## GREEN SPLIT PEA SOUP

8 oz green split peas, soaked
  overnight in plenty of cold
  water
2 onions, roughly chopped
2 pints water

1 teaspoon sea salt
1 teaspoon mixed herbs
Juice of 1 lemon
Black pepper

Yoghurt or sour cream to serve
  (optional)

Drain soaked split peas and place in a pan with 2 pints of fresh water, salt, onion and herbs. Bring to the boil and simmer, covered, for about 45 minutes until the split peas are very tender.

Liquidize the soup, then return to the pan, add lemon juice and a little black pepper, and reheat before serving.

A little yoghurt or sour cream can be added to each bowl of soup on serving.

## MIXED BEAN AND VEGETABLE SOUP

6 oz mixed dried beans and peas, such as: split peas or lentils, butter beans, haricot and other small white beans, kidney beans. Alternatively, good health food shops sell soup mixes of this type. Soak beans in cold water overnight
2 onions, roughly chopped
1 or 2 cloves garlic, crushed (optional)

2 pints water
2 vegetable stock cubes
1 teaspoon sea salt
1 tablespoon chopped parsley
1 teaspoon mixed herbs
2 large carrots, chopped
1 green pepper, chopped (optional)
2 teaspoons yeast extract
1 cup cooked grain — brown rice or other whole grain — see pages 116 and 118 (optional)

Drain soaked beans and peas and place in a pan with 2 pints fresh water, onions, garlic, vegetable stock cubes, salt and herbs. Bring to the boil, then reduce heat, cover pan and simmer gently for about 1½ hours or until all the beans and peas are tender. Add the chopped carrots and green pepper ½ hour before the end of the cooking time.

Cool slightly, then liquidize the soup. Return to the pan and add yeast extract and cooked grain if using. Season finally with sea salt and pepper to taste if necessary.

*Serve with wholemeal bread for complete meal protein.*

## CREAMY PARSNIP SOUP

¾-1 lb parsnips
2 onions
1 pint water
1 vegetable stock cube (optional)

½ pint milk
1 tablespoon parsley
1 teaspoon mixed herbs
Sea salt
1 teaspoon garam masala

Peel and roughly chop the parsnips and onions. Cover with the water, add stock cube if using, parsley, herbs and salt and bring to the boil. Simmer for about 20-30 minutes until vegetables are soft.

Liquidize the soup, then return to the pan. Add milk, garam masala and adjust seasoning to taste. Reheat and serve hot.

## LEEK AND POTATO SOUP

6 large leeks
¾ lb potatoes (approx)
1½ pints water
1 tablespoon chopped parsley
1 teaspoon mixed herbs

1 vegetable stock cube OR 1
   teaspoon yeast extract
½ pint milk
Sea salt
Black pepper
½ teaspoon nutmeg

Trim the roots from the leeks, and slice in half lengthwise. Wash in cold water then chop, using as much of the dark green as possible. Peel potatoes, wash and dice.

Bring the water to the boil, then add leeks, potatoes, herbs and stock cube or yeast extract. Simmer for about 15-20 minutes until leeks and potatoes are tender. Liquidize the soup, then return to the pan and add milk, salt and pepper to taste and nutmeg. Reheat and serve.

*For a creamier soup, add 1 or 2 tablespoons of skim milk powder to the soup before reheating.*

*Variation*
**Potato and Onion Soup**
Recipe as above but using 2 very large onions in place of leeks.

## GAZPACHO

1 onion, finely chopped
1 lb chopped tomatoes
½ cucumber, diced
2 sticks celery, chopped
½ green pepper, chopped
Parsley
1 tablespoon olive oil
Juice of 1 lemon
Sea salt and pepper
Pinch basil, marjoram,
   coriander
¾-1 pint tomato juice

Liquidize all ingredients together, in several batches if necessary. Pour into a serving bowl and chill for several hours before serving.

## BORSCH

1½ lbs cooked beetroot, (see page 56 for cooking method)
1 large potato, peeled and chopped
1 large onion, peeled and chopped
1-2 cloves garlic, crushed
1 large tomato, peeled and chopped

Yoghurt or sour cream to serve

1½ pints water
1 tablespoon parsley
½ teaspoon thyme
½ teaspoon basil
½ teaspoon marjoram
Sea salt and black pepper
1 teaspoon (approx) sugar
Juice of 1 lemon

Chop the beetroot and set to one side. Cook the potato, onion, garlic, tomato and herbs in the water for about 20 minutes or until the potato and onion are tender. Add beetroot, then liquidize the soup. Season with salt, pepper, sugar and lemon juice. Reheat, adding a little more water for a thinner soup if required.

Add 1 tablespoon of yoghurt or sour cream to each bowl of soup before serving.

*Borsch can also be served chilled in the same way.*

# Main Meals

Vegetarian main meals need a certain amount of thought and planning to ensure that the vital nutrients of life are supplied. These must, of course, include all the essential amino acids needed to build protein. The fascinating and amazingly simple trick of achieving this by correct food combining has already been explained in the section on Protein (see page 17).

For the main meals in this section those superb vegetable protein foods — pulses, nuts, seeds and whole grain, with or without the added bonus of dairy products — have been constructively put together to create complete high protein nourishment, and the resulting recipes provide interesting and varied dishes with which to inspire enthusiasm and tempt the appetite!

## WHOLEMEAL PASTRY

6 oz wholemeal flour **OR**, for
    extra protein, 4 oz whole-
    wheat flour, and 2 oz soya
    flour or wheatgerm

Pinch of sea salt
3 oz vegetable margarine
About 2 tablespoons cold
    water or milk to bind

Mix flour with salt (and soya flour or wheatgerm if using). Rub in the margarine, then add water or milk to bind and roll out on a floured board. 100% wholemeal flour does not contain as much gluten as white flour, which is why wholemeal pastry is less elastic (and less starchy) and cannot be carried over the rolling pin when rolled out! But it can be slid quite successfully from the board onto the waiting greased dish or tin, with the minimum amount of patching up needed afterwards.

Although wholemeal pastry may be more difficult to handle until accustomed to it, it is so much more nutritious and natural. And far tastier than white too. But if you do find difficulty with it, try using 85% wholemeal flour at first. This flour does not contain much bran but binds together more easily. Alternatively, use a mixture of 100% wholemeal and **unbleached strong** white flour.*

## CHEESE, ONION AND TOMATO QUICHE

6 oz *Wholemeal Pastry**, used
    to line a 9 inch flan dish

2 large onions, thinly sliced
1-2 tablespoons vegetable oil
2 tomatoes, thinly sliced
2-3 eggs

⅓ pint milk, cream or yoghurt
4 oz grated cheese
Sea salt and black pepper
½ teaspoon each oregano
    and basil

Sauté onions in oil until just tender. Arrange in the pastry case, and top with the tomato slices.

Beat eggs with milk, cream or yoghurt. Add cheese, seasoning and herbs, then pour over onion and tomato.

Bake at No.6, 400°F, for 10 minutes, then lower heat to No.4, 350°F, for 30 minutes, until firm and golden.

Serve hot or cold with vegetables or a salad.

* Use this white flour in preference to others which are over processed and chemically treated.

*Variation*
Instead of, or as well as tomato, sauté 4 oz finely chopped button mushrooms with the onion slices.

---

## COTTAGE CHEESE QUICHE

6 oz *Wholemeal Pastry*\*, used
  to line a 9 inch flan dish

8 oz *Curd Cheese*\* or cottage
  cheese
2-3 eggs
¼ pint milk, cream or
  yoghurt

2 oz grated cheese — Gruyère
  or Parmesan are good
Sea salt and black pepper
Pinch of nutmeg

Beat eggs, add cottage or *Curd*\* cheese, and milk, cream or yoghurt. Beat until thick, then stir in grated cheese, salt, pepper and nutmeg. Pour into pastry case, and bake at No.6, 400°F, for 10 minutes, then lower heat to No.4, 350°F, for about 30 minutes until set and golden.
Serve hot or cold with vegetables or a salad.

*Variation*
Finely slice an onion, and sauté in a little oil to soften. Spread over pastry case before filling.

---

## SPINACH QUICHE

6 oz *Wholemeal Pastry*\*, used
  to line a 9 inch flan dish

1 large onion, thinly sliced
1 tablespoon vegetable oil
1-2 cloves garlic, crushed
Large block of frozen
  chopped spinach, thawed
2 eggs

1 tablespoon dried parsley or
  2 tablespoons fresh
  chopped parsley
¼ pint yoghurt
4 oz grated cheese
Sea salt and black pepper
¼ teaspoon mustard

Sauté onion and garlic in oil until tender, then add spinach with parsley and cook for 5-10 minutes.
Beat eggs with yoghurt, then add cheese, seasoning and mustard. Remove spinach from heat and mix well with egg mixture. Pour

onto pastry case and bake at No.6, 400°F, for 10 minutes, then lower oven to No. 4, 350° F, for about 30 minutes, until firm and golden.
Serve hot or cold with vegetables or a salad.

*Variation*
4 oz *Curd Cheese** or cottage cheese can be used instead of hard cheese.

---

## SWEETCORN QUICHE

6 oz *Wholemeal Pastry**, used
    to line a 9 inch flan dish

| | |
|---|---|
| 1 large onion, finely chopped | ⅓ pint milk, cream or |
| 1 tablespoon vegetable oil | yoghurt |
| ½ lb packet of frozen | 4 oz grated cheese |
|    sweetcorn, or tinned | Sea salt and black pepper |
| 2 eggs | ½ teaspoon oregano |

Sauté onion in oil until tender, then arrange in the pastry case. If using frozen corn, empty packet into boiling water, bring back to the boil and then drain immediately. Alternatively, drain tinned corn. Beat together eggs and milk, cream or yoghurt, then add cheese, sweetcorn, seasoning and herbs. Pour over onion in pastry case.
Bake at No.6, 400°F, for 10 minutes, then lower oven to No.4, 350°F, for about 30 minutes until set and golden.
Serve hot or cold with vegetables or a salad.

*Variation*
Sauté 4 oz finely chopped button mushrooms with the onion.

---

## SPICY CHEESE AND LENTIL PIE FILLING

4oz small red lentils, boiled
    until tender
2 onions, finely chopped
2 cloves garlic, crushed
2 tablespoons vegetable oil
2 apples, peeled and chopped
1 teaspoon each coriander
    and cumin

Good pinch of cloves
2 teaspoons garam masala
1 tablespoon chopped parsley
Sea salt and pepper
4oz grated strong cheese
1 egg, beaten

Sauté onions and garlic in oil until transparent, then add apple.
Cook all until tender.

Add coriander, cumin and cloves and cook, stirring, for 2-3
minutes. Remove from heat, add garam masala, parsley, seasoning,
cheese, egg and drained lentils. Mix well.

### For a pie
You will need double the amount of *Wholemeal Pastry** given in
the recipe on page 100. Roll out and line a 9 inch pie dish with half
the pastry. Fill with *Spicy Cheese and Lentil Filling**, and cover
with the remaining pastry. Seal the edges and flute. Brush with
milk or a little beaten egg, and bake in the oven for 25 minutes at
No. 6, 400°F, then lower heat to No. 4, 350°F, for a further
25 minutes.

### For 4 large pasties
Use the same amount of pastry as above, but when making pasties
you may find it considerably easier to use either 85% wholemeal
flour, or a mixture of 100% wholemeal flour and **unbleached
strong** white flour. Divide the pastry into 4 and roll into ¼ inch
thick rounds. Place some filling in the centre of each round, wet the
edges of the pastry and press these lightly together to seal. Flute
the edges, lift onto a greased baking tray with a palette knife and
bake as for the pie.

### For a flan
Make enough *Wholemeal Pastry** to line a 9 inch flan dish. Fill
pastry case with filling and top with sliced tomatoes. Bake for 10
minutes at No.6, 400°F, then lower setting to No.4, 350°F for a
further 40-45 minutes until firm.

## BEAN AND VEGETABLE PIE FILLING

4 oz dried beans (use kidney, haricot, black eye, lima or a mixture of favourite beans soaked overnight in cold water
1 large onion, finely chopped
1 clove garlic, crushed
2 sticks celery, chopped
1 large carrot, grated
1 large tomato, skinned and chopped

4 oz button mushrooms, finely chopped
2 tablespoons vegetable oil
1 tablespoon soya sauce
1 tablespoon tomato purée
1 teaspoon honey
½ teaspoon each marjoram and basil
Sea salt and black pepper to taste

Bring beans to the boil with a little added salt, and simmer for 1½-2 hours until tender.

Sauté onion, garlic and celery in oil until soft, then add mushrooms, carrot, tomato and soya sauce. Cook for a few minutes then stir in tomato purée, honey, herbs, cooked drained beans and seasoning. Mix well.

### For a Pie or Pasties

Refer to previous recipe and proceed in the same way.

Alternatively, *Bean and Vegetable Pie Filling** is extremely good in wholemeal pancakes (recipe on page 106).

*Variation*

### Crispy Bean and Vegetable Bake

Spoon hot *Bean and Vegetable Pie Filling** into a shallow dish and top with a mixture of grated cheese and wholemeal breadcrumbs. Dot with a little vegetable margarine and crisp in a hot oven or under the grill.

## PIZZA

**Dough**

2 teaspoons dried yeast
1 teaspoon honey
¼ pint warm water
8 oz wholemeal flour OR use 4 oz unbleached strong

white flour, and 4 oz wholemeal flour
1 teaspoon sea salt
1 dessertspoon vegetable oil

**Topping**

1-2 large onions, finely
  chopped or sliced
1-2 cloves garlic, crushed
1-2 tablespoons vegetable oil
6-8 tomatoes, skinned and
  chopped
1 tablespoon tomato purée

½ teaspoon each basil and
  oregano
Sea salt and black pepper
4oz Bel Paese or
  Mozzarella cheese
Green or black olives and
  capers to garnish

*To make dough*
Dissolve the honey in the warm water, sprinkle the dried yeast on top and stir with a fork until dissolved. Leave in a warm place for 10-15 minutes until frothy.
Put flour and salt into a bowl, add the yeast liquid and oil, and mix to a soft dough.
Knead the dough on a lightly floured board by pulling it up at the edges and pushing it down into the middle until firm and elastic (about 5 minutes). Place in a lightly greased bowl, cover, and leave to rise in a warm place for about 45 minutes until doubled in size. Remove dough from the bowl, knead again lightly, and roll out into a large round of about 10-11 inches in diameter. Place on a greased flat tin.

*To make topping*
Sauté onion and garlic in oil until soft, then add tomatoes, tomato purée, herbs and seasoning and cook for a few minutes. Spread mixture over the top of the pizza dough covering it all, top with the cheese, grated or thinly sliced, and garnish with sliced olives and capers.
Cook pizza at No.7, 425°F, for about 20 minutes.
Serve hot with a mixed green salad.

*Variations*
Add 4oz finely sliced button mushrooms to cook with the tomatoes, or sauté 1 thinly sliced green pepper with the onion and garlic until soft. In either case, reduce the amount of onion and tomato in the topping.

# QUICK PIZZA

A quicker version can be made using a scone base for the same topping as previous recipe instead of a bread dough base.

| | |
|---|---|
| 8 oz wholemeal flour | 1-2 oz vegetable margarine |
| 2 teaspoons baking powder | 1 egg |
| Pinch of sea salt | 2-4 fluid oz milk |

In a bowl mix flour, baking powder and salt, then rub in the margarine. Make a well in the middle of the flour mixture, and break in the egg. Stir into the flour, adding enough milk to make into a soft dough. Knead lightly and press or roll out into a 10 or 11 inch round. Cover with topping and bake for 20 minutes at No. 7, 420°F.

# SAVOURY STUFFED PANCAKES

## Wholemeal Pancakes
Basic batter mixture to make 4-6 pancakes:

| | |
|---|---|
| 4 oz wholemeal flour | ½ pint of milk, water, or |
| Pinch of sea salt | a mixture of both |
| 1 egg | Vegetable oil for frying |

Mix flour and salt together in a bowl, make a well in the centre and break the egg into it with a little of the milk and/or water. Gradually mix the flour into the egg and milk, adding the rest of the liquid as the mixture thickens. When all the flour has been mixed in, beat the mixture until smooth. Allow to stand for at least ½ hour if possible. To cook pancakes, heat a little oil in a frying pan until very hot, then swirl enough pancake mixture around the pan to cover thinly.
Turn pancakes when cooked on one side, and when both sides are golden brown, slide onto a plate and keep warm in a slow oven until ready to fill.

*Variation*

## Enriched Soya Pancakes
Make pancakes as before, but use half soya flour and half wholewheat flour. The protein of the soya and wheat complement

each other, and make these pancakes more nutritious as well as very tasty.

For a quick savoury stuffed pancake meal, fill with grated cheese. And sautéd onion, garlic and cooked or canned vegetables such as sweetcorn, asparagus, mushrooms, etc, are all ideal as quick pancake fillings. Roll up, cover with slices of cheese for protein, brown under the grill and serve with a salad.

Pancakes can be made in advance, cooled, and kept wrapped in a fridge until needed. Then fill with required filling, and place in a greased oven dish. Cover and heat in a moderate oven.

Alternatively, rolled-up stuffed pancakes are delicious and unusual when covered in a *Cheese Sauce*\* and baked for about 1/2 hour until sauce is golden and bubbling.

---

## PANCAKES WITH PEANUT BUTTER
## AND COTTAGE CHEESE

*Pancakes*\*

**Filling**

1 onion, finely chopped
1 tablespoon vegetable oil
1 eating apple, peeled and
  chopped

2 tomatoes, skinned and
  chopped
8 oz cottage cheese
1 dessertspoon sweet pickle
2 tablespoons peanut butter

Sauté onion in oil until tender, then add apple and tomatoes and cook for a few minutes to soften. Add cottage cheese, pickle and peanut butter, mix well and heat through.

Make *Pancakes*\* and spread each one with some filling. Roll up and keep warm in a slow oven until all the pancakes are ready to be served. Serve with a green salad.

---

## PANCAKES WITH SPINACH AND CURD CHEESE
*Pancakes\**

### Filling
| | |
|---|---|
| 1 onion, thinly sliced | 1 teaspoon dried mixed herbs |
| 1-2 cloves garlic, crushed | 8oz *Curd Cheese\** (cottage |
| 1 tablespoon vegetable oil | cheese or cream cheese |
| ½lb packet frozen chopped | could be used instead, and |
| or puréed spinach, thawed | are equally good) |
| 1 tablespoon chopped parsley | Sea salt and black pepper |

Sauté onion and garlic in oil until soft, then add spinach and cook for 5-10 minutes, stirring occasionally. Add herbs, salt and pepper and finally cheese. Mix well and heat through briefly without boiling. Make *Pancakes\** and roll up some filling in each. Serve immediately or keep warm in a low oven. Accompany with a side salad.

*Variation*
### Spinach Pancakes
Recipe as above but omit cheese or other type and double the quantity of spinach. 1 or 2 tablespoons of soured cream could be added after cooking if wished.
Roll up *Pancakes\** and cover each with a slice of Mozzarella cheese. Brown quickly under a hot grill before serving.

## PANCAKES WITH PROVENÇALE FILLING
*Pancakes\**

### Provençale Filling
| | |
|---|---|
| 2 large onions, finely sliced | 2 tablespoons tomato purée |
| 2 cloves garlic, crushed | 1 teaspoon honey |
| 1 tablespoon vegetable oil | Sea salt and black pepper |
| 4oz button mushrooms, thinly sliced | ½ teaspoon each basil and oregano |
| 4 tomatoes, skinned and chopped | 1 teaspoon chopped parsley |
| | 6oz grated cheese |

Sauté onion and garlic in oil until tender. Add mushrooms and cook for a few minutes before adding tomatoes, tomato purée, honey, seasoning and herbs. Simmer gently for 5 minutes. Make *Pancakes\**, spread each one with some filling, and sprinkle with grated cheese. Roll up and place in a greased shallow oven dish. Heat quickly in a very hot oven to melt the cheese, then serve immediately accompanied with a green salad.

*Variation*
Finely chopped aubergine can be added to sauté with the onion and garlic. But note that quantities of other vegetables could be reduced.

## CHINESE-STYLE PANCAKES

*Pancakes\**

1 medium onion, finely sliced
1 red pepper, sliced
4oz button mushrooms, sliced
1-2 tablespoons vegetable oil

4oz bean sprouts
1 tablespoon soya sauce
2oz sliced toasted almonds
Sea salt and black pepper

Sauté onion, pepper and mushrooms in oil until tender, then add bean sprouts with soya sauce. Cover pan and steam for a few minutes until bean sprouts are just cooked but still crisp. Stir in almond slices, salt and pepper, and fill prepared *Pancakes\**.
Place rolled up pancakes finally into a very hot oven for 5-10 minutes to allow them to crispen on the outside, Chinese style!

## SOYA NUT PANCAKES WITH CREAMED MUSHROOMS

**For the pancake batter**

| | |
|---|---|
| 3 oz soya flour | ⅓ pint milk |
| 3 oz finely ground mixed nuts | 1 tablespoon soya sauce |
| 2 eggs | ½ teaspoon mixed herbs |

**For the creamed mushrooms**

| | |
|---|---|
| 8 oz button mushrooms, finely chopped | ¾ pint milk |
| 2 oz vegetable margarine | 1 tablespoon chopped parsley |
| 2 oz wholemeal flour | Sea salt and pepper |

Mix the soya flour and ground nuts together and use in place of flour to make the pancake batter as on page 106. To cook, spread batter fairly generously around the hot, oiled frying pan to make slightly thicker pancakes, and cook them more slowly. Take care when turning the pancakes that they do not get broken.

When all the pancakes are made keep them warm, covered, in a low oven. To make the filling, sauté chopped mushrooms in the vegetable margarine until just tender, then add the flour and stir until frothy. Remove from the heat and add milk, then return to heat and stir until thick and smooth. Add parsley, salt and pepper to taste. To serve, place some creamed mushroom filling onto each pancake, and fold the pancakes around it. Serve immediately with a side salad.

*Variation*

Leeks could be used instead of mushrooms to make the creamed filling. Or try sweetcorn, adding cooked or tinned kernels to the white sauce after it has thickened.

## SPANISH OMELETTE

| | |
|---|---|
| 4-6 eggs, beaten together | 1 red pepper, finely chopped |
| 1 large spanish onion, finely chopped | 2 tablespoons olive oil |
| 1-2 cloves garlic, crushed | 4 tomatoes, skinned and chopped |
| 1 green pepper, finely chopped | 1-2 large potatoes, cooked and diced |

Sauté onion, garlic and peppers in oil, and cook gently until soft. Add tomatoes and cooked potato, and heat through, stirring. Pour the egg mixture over cooking vegetables, and stir gently to distribute the egg. When the underside of the omelette is cooked but the top still runny, lower heat, clamp on lid, and leave for 2-3 minutes or until the top has set and begun to 'rise' in the pan. Do not fold, but divide into portions and scoop out flat onto heated plates.

---

## CHEESE SOUFFLÉ

3 oz vegetable margarine  
3 oz wholemeal flour  
¾ pint milk  
6 oz grated cheese  

4 eggs, separated  
½ teaspoon mustard powder (optional)  
Sea salt and black pepper  

Melt margarine in a pan, then add the flour and cook, stirring until frothy. Remove from the heat and stir in the milk. Bring to the boil stirring until the mixture is thick and smooth. Allow to cool slightly then add cheese, egg yolks, mustard and seasonings. Whisk the egg whites until stiff and fold them into the cheese mixture. Pour into a well greased soufflé dish and bake at No.4, 350°F, for about 45 minutes.

Serve on its own or with a *Tomato** or *Wine Sauce**, and accompany with a side salad and baked or boiled potatoes.

*Variations*

**Nut Soufflé**
As for *Cheese Soufflé** but use 4 oz ground mixed nuts instead of cheese, and add a good pinch of herbs instead of mustard powder. Bake and serve as above.

**Mushroom Soufflé**
Sauté 8 oz finely chopped button mushrooms in the vegetable margarine before adding the flour. Proceed as above but omit cheese and add a teaspoon of mixed herbs.

---

## CHEESE SOUFFLÉ WITH SEMOLINA

¾ pint milk
2oz wholewheat semolina
4 eggs, separated

6oz grated cheese
Sea salt and black pepper

Warm the milk slightly, then sprinkle in the semolina. Bring to the boil, stirring all the time, and cook gently for about 3 minutes. Remove from heat, and allow to cool a bit before adding egg yolks, grated cheese, salt and pepper.
Stiffly beat the egg whites, and fold into the semolina mixture. Pour into a greased soufflé dish and bake for ¾-1 hour at No.4, 350°F. Serve immediately with a side salad or vegetables.
*The soufflé could also be accompanied by a Tomato\* or Wine Sauce\* if wished.*

## WHOLEWHEAT SPAGHETTI

Allow 2-3oz raw spaghetti (or other pasta) per person. Place in boiling salted water and cook, stirring occasionally to separate, until tender — about 15 minutes. Serve with any of the following pasta sauces:

### Italian Tomato Sauce

1-2 large onions, peeled and thinly sliced
1-2 cloves garlic, crushed
½ green pepper, seeded and sliced
4oz button mushrooms, sliced
1 tablespoon vegetable oil
15-oz can tomatoes
Sea salt and black pepper

2 bay leaves
1 teaspoon each basil and oregano
1 tablespoon parsley
2 tablespoons tomato purée
1 teaspoon yeast extract
1 teaspoon honey
Dash red wine (optional)
Pine nuts and chopped olives can be added to sauce

Sauté onion, garlic and pepper in oil. Add mushrooms and stir until vegetables are tender.
Add all other ingredients and simmer gently for 5-10 minutes. Serve on wholewheat spaghetti or noodles, and top with grated cheese or chopped nuts. Accompany with a green salad.

## Aubergine and Tomato Sauce

As above, but use only 1 onion and add 1 large aubergine which has been chopped, salted and left for about ½ hour, then rinsed and drained. Sauté with onion, garlic and pepper. Mushrooms could be omitted from sauce.

## Mock Bolognese Sauce

To either of the above, after sautéing the vegetables, add ½ pint water, 1 vegetable stock cube and 4oz textured vegetable protein mince (TVP). Add the remaining ingredients at the same time, and simmer as before for 5-10 minutes. Serve on wholewheat spaghetti for a lovely Spaghetti Bolognese dish. Accompany with grated Parmesan cheese and a green salad.

---

# LASAGNE

8oz wholewheat lasagne
  pasta

Pasta sauce: *Italian Tomato*    *Tomato Sauce**
*Sauce**, Auber-*    or *Mock Bolog-*
*gine and*    *nese Sauce**

1 pint *White Sauce**
6-8oz grated cheese — use a
  strong Cheddar

Cook lasagne in a large pan of boiling salted water for 15-20 minutes, adding a piece at a time to prevent them sticking. Stir gently occasionally. Drain and rinse with hot water.

Grease a large shallow ovenproof dish and cover the bottom with half of the *White Sauce**. On to this place a few sheets of lasagne and cover thinly with a little pasta sauce. Sprinkle with some grated cheese. Continue layers of pasta, sauce and grated cheese, finishing with a pasta layer and retaining some grated cheese for the topping. Cover with the rest of the *White Sauce** and sprinkle with remaining grated cheese.

Bake at No.4, 350°F for 30-40 minutes until golden.

Serve with a tossed green side salad.

### Nut Lasagne
As above, but use 4-6oz of ground or finely chopped nuts instead of cheese in the layers. Top with a little grated Parmesan cheese to finish and cook as above.

### Bean and Aubergine Lasagne
Method as above but use *Beans and Aubergine in Wine** on page 130 for the pasta sauce.

### Spinach Lasagne
Method as before, but use the spinach filling as given for *Spinach Pancakes**, on page 108 in place of any of the pasta sauces. Make a richly flavoured *Cheese Sauce** instead of the *White Sauce** used in the other lasagne recipes, and omit the grated cheese from the layers. A little grated Parmesan cheese is a very good substitute if you wish. Cook as before.

---

## MACARONI CHEESE

6oz wholewheat macaroni, cooked in boiling water until tender
1 large onion, thinly sliced
1 green pepper, seeded and thinly sliced
2 tablespoons vegetable oil
2 tablespoons wholemeal flour
1 pint milk
6oz grated cheese
4oz button mushrooms, washed and finely chopped
1 small can sweetcorn, drained
2-3 hard boiled eggs, chopped
Sea salt and black pepper
Dash of tabasco
Pinch of mixed herbs
2-3 sliced tomatoes to garnish

In a large pan sauté onion and pepper slices in oil until soft. Add flour and stir until bubbling. Remove from heat and stir in the milk, then return to heat and bring to the boil stirring all the time until smooth and thick. Add the mushrooms and cook gently for a few minutes. Remove from heat and stir in all the other ingredients except the tomatoes. Transfer into a shallow greased oven dish, top with sliced tomatoes, and place in a hot oven for 10-15 minutes to heat through.

*This dish can be made in advance and heated up in the oven when needed.*

## GNOCCI

1 pint of milk
4 oz wholewheat semolina
1 oz vegetable margarine
4 oz grated cheese
1 egg, beaten

Sea salt and black pepper
*Italian Tomato Sauce** or
*Aubergine and Tomato
Sauce** to serve

Heat the milk, and then sprinkle in the semolina. Stirring all the time, bring to the boil, and cook gently for a few minutes until thickened. Remove from the heat and add the margarine, half the cheese, and the beaten egg. Mix well and stir over a low heat without boiling, for 1 minute.

Spread evenly onto a large flat, wetted or oiled dish, to about ½ inch in depth thick. Leave to stand until cold, then cut into 1-inch squares and arrange overlapping in rows in a shallow greased oven dish. Sprinkle with the rest of the grated cheese, and bake in a hot oven or under a medium grill for about 15 minutes until hot and golden.

Serve with *Italian Tomato Sauce** or *Aubergine and Tomato Sauce** and a green salad.

---

## SPINACH, NOODLES AND CHEESE

8 oz wholewheat noodles,
  cooked until tender
1 large packet frozen
  chopped spinach
1 large onion, finely sliced
1 clove garlic, crushed
1 teaspoon mixed herbs
1 teaspoon sea salt
Ground black pepper

Pinch nutmeg
Vegetable oil
8 oz *Curd Cheese** or cottage
  cheese
¼ pint yoghurt mixed with 2
  tablespoons skim milk
  powder
2 eggs, beaten
2 oz grated Cheddar cheese

Thaw spinach and cook in a little vegetable oil for 5-10 minutes. Meanwhile sauté onion and garlic in about 1 tablespoon vegetable oil until tender, then add cooked spinach and herbs and stir gently over heat for 1 minute. Season mixture finally with salt, pepper and nutmeg. Beat together egg, *Curd Cheese** or cottage cheese, and yoghurt with skim milk powder. Alternatively, this mixture can be blended in a liquidizer for a smoother result.

Fold cooked noddles into egg and cheese mixture, add spinach and onions and mix all together. Pile into a greased oven dish, sprinkle with the grated cheese and cover with a lid or foil. Bake at No.4, 350°F, for 10 minutes until firm, then remove lid or foil and return to oven for another 10 minutes to brown the cheese topping. Serve on its own or with *Italian Tomato Sauce**.

## BROWN RICE

Brown rice is a wonderfully nutritious food. A good source of protein, and rich in the B vitamins as well as other essential vitamins and minerals, this cereal should play an important part in a healthy vegetarian diet. Polished white rice, in comparison, has had most of the nutritive value removed during milling and processing, and I think most of the flavour as well.

Use any type of unpolished brown rice, available from health food shops. Allow 2-3 oz of uncooked rice for each adult portion, and 2-$2\frac{1}{2}$ times the volume of water; the more cooking water used, the softer the grains of rice will be.

Sea salt

Wash the rice well in plenty of cold water, and drain in a sieve. Bring the cooking water, with a little sea salt added, to the boil in a pan with a tight fitting lid. Then add the rice slowly so that the water does not stop boiling. Cover the pan, lower the heat and simmer very gently for about $\frac{3}{4}$ hour, or until all the water has been absorbed and the rice is tender. With some types of brown rice this may take longer. If the rice is still not sufficiently cooked after the water has been absorbed, a little more boiling water should be added to the pan. Cook as before until absorbed. But rice should never be stirred during cooking as this encourages it to become soggy and unappetizing. Empty the cooked rice into a large sieve, and pour fresh boiling water over it to wash away any excess starch. This final rinsing results in fluffy light rice with the grains separate. Drain well and serve immediately, or keep warm in a covered dish in the oven.

*For a savoury taste, add 1 tablespoon of soya sauce or a vegetable stock cube to the cooking water. For extra protein, add 1 tablespoon of soya splits per 4 oz uncooked rice, to cook with the rice.*

*Cooked rice keeps well in the fridge for several days.*

## SAVOURY RICE WITH HERBS

8oz brown rice, cooked in 1¼ pints of boiling water according to recommended cooking instructions opposite, with about ½ teaspoon each of dried marjoram, rosemary and thyme, or other dried herbs to taste.

1 large onion, finely chopped
1-2 cloves garlic, crushed
1 tablespoon vegetable oil
1 teaspoon turmeric
1 tablespoon chopped fresh parsley
Other chopped fresh herbs as available
Sea salt and black pepper

Sauté onion and garlic in oil until soft.
Add turmeric, rice, herbs and seasoning, and mix up well. Heat through before serving.

*Variation*
4oz button mushrooms could be sautéd with the onion and garlic.

**Tomato Savoury Rice**
As either of the above, but instead of turmeric add 1 tablespoon each of tomato purée and soya sauce, and add 4 skinned and chopped tomatoes.

*And for a quick protein dish toss into either savoury rice about 4oz sunflower seeds or roasted peanuts, and serve with a side salad. Complete the meal with yoghurt to provide calcium, and fresh fruit.*

## MAIN MEAL SAVOURY RICE

8 oz brown rice
2 tablespoons soya splits
(optional)

1¼ pints water
1 teaspoon sea salt
1 tablespoon soya sauce

Cook rice, and soya splits if using, in boiling water with salt and soya sauce (see rice cooking method on page 116).

1 large onion, thinly sliced
1 green pepper, seeded and
thinly sliced
1 tablespoon vegetable oil
4 oz button mushrooms,
thinly sliced
6 oz approximately, lightly
precooked vegetables such
as peas, sweetcorn, cauliflower florettes, carrots

2 oz sunflower seeds, pine
nuts or roasted peanuts
2 hard boiled eggs, chopped
(optional)
Sea salt and black pepper
Herbs — parsley, thyme,
rosemary, marjoram, or
others to taste as available

Sauté onion and pepper slices in oil until tender. Add mushrooms, and cook for a few minutes before adding cooked rice, vegetables and all other ingredients. Mix lightly while heating through. Serve immediately or keep warm in a covered heatproof dish in a low oven.

## WHOLE GRAINS

There's no need to stop at brown rice! Other grains will provide a wide variety of taste and nutrients for the vegetarian and whole food enthusiast alike, and these can be cooked using the same method, and served in the same ways as rice. Try millet, whole wheat, rye and barley to replace rice in any of the *Savoury Rice** dishes; or mix together a selection of cooked whole grains. Discover cracked (or kibbled) wheat which is the whole grain broken up to make it easier to cook; and bulgar cracked wheat, a Middle Eastern dish, which has been partly cooked and treated with milk before being dried and broken up.

Although the same cooking rules apply for all these whole grains as given for brown rice, the amounts of water and the cooking times they all require varies slightly with each grain:

| Rye | Cook in 3 times its volume of water for about 2 hours |
| Millet | Cook in 3 times its volume of water for about 30 minutes |
| Barley (pot barley is the whole grain) | Cook in 3 times its volume of water for about 1¼ hours |
| Whole Wheat | Cook in 3 times its volume of water for about 2 hours |
| Cracked Wheat | Cook in twice its volume of water for 20-30 minutes |
| Bulgar | Cook in twice its volume of water for about 15 minutes |

The suggested cooking times for whole grains and the amounts of water estimated are, of course, approximate. All grains must be cooked very slowly in a covered pan, without stirring, until the liquid is absorbed and the grain tender. More boiling water may have to be added to the pan if the grain still seems undercooked after the full cooking time.

---

## MILLET PILAF

1 large onion, finely chopped
1 green pepper, finely chopped
1 or 2 cloves garlic, crushed (optional)
2 tablespoons vegetable oil
1½ pints water
1 teaspoon thyme
2 bay leaves

1 tablespoon parsley
1 teaspoon sea salt
1-2 vegetable stock cubes
8 oz whole hulled millet
4 tablespoons yoghurt
2 oz pine nuts or chopped almonds
2 oz raisins (optional)

Sauté onions, pepper and garlic in the oil until soft. Add the water, herbs, salt and vegetable stock cube and bring to the boil before then adding the millet. Return to the boil, stirring once, then lower the heat and cook very gently, covered, for 30 minutes. After this time, if the millet is tender but still appears too wet, remove the lid and simmer (without stirring) for a few minutes until the excess liquid evaporates. Remove from the heat and stir in yoghurt, nuts and raisins.

Serve Millet Pilaf with another dish or serve on its own sprinkled with grated cheese and accompanied by a side salad.

*Variation*
**Cracked Wheat or Bulgar Pilaf**
Pilaf can be made as the recipe above, using cracked wheat or bulgar wheat instead of millet, but these will need only 1¼ pints water. For Bulgar Pilaf, reduce the cooking time to about 15 minutes, omit the raisins and, if you like, add the juice of ½ lemon finally, to bring out the fresh tangy taste of the bulgar.

## CURRY SAUCE

| | |
|---|---|
| 1 onion, finely chopped or grated | 2 tablespoons wholemeal flour |
| 1 clove garlic, crushed | 1 pint water |
| 2 apples, peeled and finely chopped OR 1 apple and 1 or 2 peeled and chopped parsnips | 1-2 vegetable stock cubes |
| | Juice of ½ lemon |
| | 1-2 teaspoons of honey to taste |
| 2 tablespoons vegetable oil | 1 bay leaf |
| 1 tablespoon curry powder | Sea salt and pepper |

Sauté onion, garlic, apples and parsnips if using, in oil until tender. Add curry powder and flour and cook, stirring for a few minutes. Add water and remaining ingredients, and stir over heat until thick. Simmer covered for 15 minutes. Remove bay leaf before serving, and if desired the sauce can be liquidized or passed through a food strainer for a smoother texture.

For a quick curry meal, serve Curry Sauce poured over *Savoury Rice\** or other grain, with added nuts or seeds to make up complete protein. Accompany with curry side dishes and a green salad.

*Curry Sauce is an ideal base for many curry ideas, and I have included a few favourites here. It is also a marvellous way of using up left-over vegetables which can be thrown into the sauce at the last minute, and the resulting super-quick vegetable curry served with Brown Rice\*. Provide a side dish of peanuts or cashews to complement the protein in the rice and so supply complete protein nourishment. Alternatively serve yoghurt in the meal, either for pudding or with the curry as a side dish.*

## CURRIES

**Egg Curry**
To *Curry Sauce*\*, add 1 hard boiled egg per person and simmer gently for about 5 minutes. Serve with boiled *Brown Rice*\* and curry side dishes (see page 123) and accompany with a green salad.

**Banana and Nut Curry**
To *Curry Sauce*\* add for each person, 1 thickly sliced banana, 1 oz any nuts roasted in a hot oven or under the grill, and 1 oz raisins. Cook for a few minutes. Serve with *Brown Rice*\* and side dishes of poppadoms, sweet chutney and yoghurt.

**Lentil Curry**
Soak and cook about 6-8 oz lentils (or other pulse such as soya beans or chick peas) and add to *Curry Sauce*\* with 2-3 oz raisins. If possible, the cooking liquid from the lentils should be reserved, made up to 1 pint, and used for the *Curry Sauce*\*. Serve with *Brown Rice*\* and curry side dishes to increase food value. Or serve with a *Rice and Nut Mould*\* and a side salad.

## INDIAN VEGETABLE CURRY

About 1 lb raw vegetables:
  Carrots, peeled and diced
  Cauliflower florettes
  Celery, thinly sliced
  Peas
  Sweetcorn
1 onion, peeled and finely
  sliced
1 clove garlic, crushed
1 eating apple, chopped
2 tablespoons vegetable oil
2 teaspoons turmeric

2 teaspoons coriander
1 teaspoon cumin
1 teaspoon ginger
¼ teaspoon chilli powder
Pinch cloves
¾ pint water
Sea salt and ground black
  pepper
Juice of 1 lemon
1 tablespoon honey
2 teaspoons garam masala
¼ pint natural yoghurt

Sauté onion, garlic and apple in oil until tender.
Add turmeric, coriander, cumin, ginger, chilli powder and cloves, and cook very slowly for a few minutes, stirring all the while. Stir in water and bring to the boil. Lower heat and cook very gently for about 5 minutes before adding vegetables.
Simmer for 10 minutes, then add garam masala, lemon juice, honey, salt and pepper to taste, and finally yoghurt. Stir and heat, but do not boil. Serve immediately with *Brown Rice**.

A selection of the following side dishes should be passed around at the table in small bowls, and sprinkled to taste on the curry: peanuts or other nuts, raisins, coconut, poppadoms, chutney, *Yoghurt and Cucumber Salad**, *Dahl**.

*If not serving Dahl**, *be sure to serve peanuts or cashew nuts as a side dish to complement the rice protein. Yoghurt and Cucumber Salad** *provides calcium and some extra milk protein too.*

## DAHL

This is an Indian vegetable dish made here with split peas. For a typical Indian meal, serve with *Brown Rice** with or without a *Vegetable Curry** and some curry side dishes. Alternatively serve with wholemeal bread. The protein in the split peas and brown rice or bread, complement each other and make a nutritious and tasty meal.

| 8oz split peas | 1 teaspoon sea salt |

Soak split peas in plenty of cold water, overnight or for a couple of hours at least. Then bring to the boil with the salt and simmer for 30-50 minutes until tender. Drain, reserving liquid.

| 2 onions, finely chopped | Pinch ground cloves |
| 2 tablespoons vegetable oil | Sea salt and black pepper |
| 2 teaspoons turmeric | 1 teaspoon honey |
| 1 teaspoon coriander | Juice of 1 lemon |
| 1 teaspoon cumin | 2 teaspoons garam masala |

Sauté onion slowly in oil until transparent. Add turmeric, coriander, cumin and cloves and cook very slowly for 5 minutes, stirring.

Add cooked split peas and some of the cooking liquid. Dahl should be thick but still able to be poured onto rice.

Cook slowly for about 10 minutes.

Add garam masala, honey and lemon juice, and allow to stand for a while. Reheat before serving and add salt to taste.

*Dahl is also very good eaten cold with a side salad.*

---

**Side Dishes for Curry**
Peanuts or other nuts
Coconut — desiccated or grated fresh
Chopped hard boiled eggs
Chopped apples
Sliced bananas
Chopped tomatoes
Chopped green peppers
Raisins or other dried fruit
Poppadoms
Sweet chutney
*Yoghurt and Cucumber Salad*\*
Yoghurt
Buttermilk to drink is cooling and quite delicious

Dishes containing any of the above, passed around the table to sprinkle on curry, add flavour, food value and of course atmosphere to a curry meal. Try to provide the ones that will enhance the flavour of whatever curry is being served.

---

## VEGETABLE KEBABS

**On skewers, pierce**

Chunks of aubergine
Whole small onions, or larger
    onions halved or quartered
Pieces of green and/or
    red peppers

Chunks of cucumber or
    courgette
Tomatoes
Mushrooms
Cubes of pineapple

**Basting Sauce**

2 tablespoons vegetable oil
2 tablespoons sherry, white
    wine or cider
Sea salt and pepper
Crushed garlic cloves
Juice of 1 lemon

1-2 tablespoons tomato purée
1 teaspoon honey
Herbs — rosemary, basil and
    thyme or others as
    available

Mix all sauce ingredients together.
Grill the skewered vegetables slowly until tender, basting
frequently with the sauce.
Serve kebabs on a bed of *Savoury Rice\** or other grain, with added
nuts or sunflower seeds for protein, and with the basting sauce
spooned over. Alternatively serve with a *Rice and Nut Mould\** or
*Millet Pilaf\**.

## CHINESE RICE

6 oz brown rice
2 tablespoons soya splits
    (optional — alternatively
    use 8 oz rice)

1¼ pints boiling water
½ teaspoon sea salt
1 tablespoon soya sauce

Cook rice, and soya splits if being used, in the boiling water with
salt and soya sauce until water is absorbed and rice tender (see rice
cooking method on page 116).

1 large onion, thinly sliced
1 red or green pepper, seeded
    and thinly sliced
1 clove garlic, crushed
2 sticks celery, sliced
    diagonally

3 oz blanched almonds, split
    and toasted until golden
    under a grill
Shredded omelette, made
    with 2 eggs
2 tablespoons vegetable oil

4 oz button mushrooms,
washed and thinly sliced
4 oz bean sprouts, fresh or
tinned
8 oz chopped pineapple, fresh
or tinned

1 tablespoon soya sauce, or
more to taste
1 teaspoon ginger (optional)

Prepare all ingredients before you start. The secret of good Chinese Rice is the speed of cooking which results in crispy vegetables. Heat oil in a large frying pan and briefly fry onion, pepper, garlic and celery until only just beginning to soften, stirring all the time. Add mushrooms, bean sprouts and soya sauce, stir over heat for a minute, then add pineapple, almonds, ground ginger if using, and cooked rice. Heat, stirring until rice is hot, then pile onto a warmed serving dish. Arrange omelette pieces on top and serve.

---

## SPICY CHICK PEAS WITH RICE

4 oz chick peas, soaked
overnight in plenty of cold
water
8 oz brown rice
2 onions, chopped
1 clove garlic, crushed
2 tablespoons vegetable oil

4 oz button mushrooms,
chopped
4 tomatoes, skinned and
chopped
2 teaspoons garam masala
1 teaspoon turmeric
Sea salt and pepper

Cook chick peas in the same water that they were soaked in, with 1 teaspoon sea salt added, for about 2 hours, or until tender. Drain. Cook the rice in 1¼ pints boiling salted water until tender (see rice cooking method on page 116).
Sauté onions and garlic in oil, then add mushrooms and cook for a few minutes until all are tender. Add garam masala and turmeric and stir briefly over a low heat. Add tomatoes, cooked and drained chick peas, cooked rice and seasoning to taste. Heat through, stirring, then serve hot with a green salad.

---

## FRUIT AND NUT MOULD

8 oz brown rice                    1 teaspoon sea salt
1¼ pints water

Cook rice in boiling water with salt as cooking method for *Brown Rice** but there is no need to give the cooked rice a final rinsing for this recipe.

2 oz dried apricots or figs,       2 oz raisins
  split and chopped

Place the fruits in a small bowl, just cover them in boiling water and leave for several hours to soak.

4 oz altogether of hazelnuts, pine nuts, cashew nuts and almonds

Rough chop nuts and roast for a few minutes under the grill or in a hot oven.

1 large onion, finely chopped      1 dessertspoon wholemeal
1 tablespoon vegetable oil           flour
1 teaspoon turmeric                ¼ pint of milk
½ teaspoon coriander or            Sea salt and ground black
  cumin                              pepper

Sauté onion in oil until tender. Add turmeric, spice and flour and cook for a few minutes, stirring. Pour in milk and stir over heat until thick. Add soaked fruit and any juice there may be left from the soaking, chopped roasted nuts and cooked rice.
Heat through and season to taste.
Press into a well oiled heated ring or mould. Keep warm in the oven until needed if necessary, then turn onto a warmed dish and serve immediately accompanied with a smooth *Curry Sauce** and a green salad.

   *This is a very attractive and wonderfully flavoured dish, and the combined nuts and rice make it a good protein one too.*

*Variation*
Add 1-2 teaspoons curry powder with the turmeric and coriander. Serve with a bowl of warmed yoghurt to spoon over each portion and a cool green salad.

**Rice and Nut Mould**
As for the *Fruit and Nut Rice Mould\** but omit the fruit. This version is an ideal protein accompaniment to another dish such as *Vegetable Kebabs\**, or just serve on its own with *Yoghurt and Cucumber Salad\**.

## CORN, MILLET AND NUT BAKE

4 oz hulled millet
¾ pint water
1 teaspoon sea salt
1 onion, peeled and finely chopped
1 eating apple, peeled and chopped
2 eggs
⅓ pint yoghurt
1 tablespoon chopped parsley

½ teaspoon each of sage and thyme
Dash of Worcestershire sauce
Sea salt and ground black pepper
½ lb sweetcorn — if frozen, cook in boiling water for 1 minute; or use tinned
4 oz peanuts or cashew nuts, ground

Add millet slowly to rapidly boiling water to avoid lumping. Cover tightly with pan lid and cook for about 30 minutes or until water is absorbed and millet tender.
Meanwhile, sauté onion in oil until transparent, then add apple and cook for a few minutes to soften. Remove from heat.
Beat eggs and yoghurt together with herbs and seasoning. Add to the cooked onions and apple together with drained sweetcorn, ground nuts and cooked millet. Mix all the ingredients well.
Turn into a greased shallow oven dish, top with tomato slices and bake at No.4, 350°F for 45 minutes until firm and golden.

## BROWN LENTILS

8 oz brown lentils. Wash
these and soak overnight
or longer in cold water
1 onion, finely chopped
1 clove garlic, crushed

1 tablespoon vegetable oil
1 teaspoon coriander
Sea salt and black pepper
Juice of ½ lemon

In a large pan sauté the onion and garlic briefly in vegetable oil. Add coriander, stir over heat for a minute, then add lentils and about ½ pint water. Bring to the boil, removing any scum. Season with approximately ½ teaspoon salt and some black pepper. Cover the pan and simmer gently for about 1-1½ hours until very tender. A little more boiling water may be added if the lentils get too dry. Add lemon juice finally and thicken with ¼ pint sour cream, yoghurt, or a flour and milk mixture (mix approximately 1 dessertspoon of flour to a smooth paste with a little milk taken from ¼ pint. Stir in the remainder of the milk, add this to lentils and stir until thick).

Adjust seasoning before serving.

Serve with *Brown Rice**, other cooked grain, or just on wholemeal toast for a complete protein dish. Alternatively, *Brown Lentils** are delicious served with baked potatoes, grated cheese and a side salad.

## LENTIL AND CHEESE CASSEROLE

6 oz small red lentils
2 large onions, peeled and
thinly sliced
4 oz button mushrooms,
washed and sliced
½ lb tomatoes, skinned and
sliced

½ pint milk
6 oz grated Cheddar cheese
1 egg
3 oz wholemeal breadcrumbs
1 teaspoon mixed herbs
Sea salt and black pepper

Grease a casserole dish and place the onion, tomato and mushroom slices on the bottom.

Cover with lentils.

Mix together breadcrumbs, cheese, milk, egg, salt, pepper and herbs, and then pour mixture over the lentils.

Bake at No.4, 350°F for about 1½ hours.

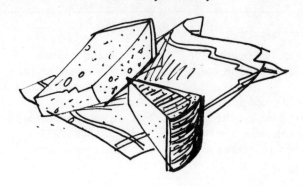

## CORN AND CHICK PEA CRUMBLE

4 oz chick peas, soaked
overnight in plenty of cold
water
½ lb packet frozen sweetcorn
1 large onion
1 clove garlic, crushed
4 oz button mushrooms,
chopped

2 tablespoons vegetable oil
1 tablespoon tomato purée
½ teaspoon yeast extract
Sea salt and black pepper
½ teaspoon chopped
rosemary
1 tablespoon chopped parsley

Crumble:  3 oz wholemeal
breadcrumbs
3 oz grated cheese

Vegetable
margarine

Boil the chick peas in the same water they were soaked in, with 1
teaspoon of sea salt, for about 2 hours or until tender. Drain,
conserving cooking water. Purée chick peas in a blender or through
a food mincer, adding enough of the cooking water to make it
easier to purée, and to result in a thick dropping consistency (a bit
like mashed potato!). Put to one side. Plunge sweetcorn into a pan
of boiling water, return to the boil, then immediately drain.
Sauté onion and garlic in oil until soft, add mushrooms and cook
for a few minutes, then add all other ingredients, including chick
pea purée and sweetcorn. Stir well. Pile into a greased oven dish.
Mix breadcrumbs with grated cheese, and sprinkle over chick pea
mixture. Dot with vegetable margarine and place in a hot oven
until bubbling hot and the crumble crisp.

## BEAN HOT POT

6 oz dried mixed beans,
  soaked overnight in cold
  water
1 large onion, chopped
  1 clove garlic, crushed
2 large carrots, chopped
1 tablespoon vegetable oil
2 x 15 oz cans tomatoes

Sea salt and pepper
1 teaspoon yeast extract
½ teaspoon each marjoram
  and basil
1½ lbs potatoes, peeled and
  thinly sliced
A little vegetable margarine

Bring beans to the boil with a little salt added, and simmer until all are tender. This will take approximately 1-2½ hours.
Sauté onion, garlic and carrots in the oil until tender. Stir in the yeast extract to dissolve, then add herbs, tomatoes and cooked drained beans.
Season to taste.
Transfer to a greased casserole dish, top with the sliced potato and sprinkle with salt and pepper. Dot potato with vegetable margarine. Cover with lid or foil and cook at No.4, 350°F, for 2 hours. Remove lid for the last 30 minutes to allow potatoes to brown.

---

## BEANS AND AUBERGINE IN WINE

6 oz altogether of red
  kidney beans, butter (or
  lima) beans and haricot
  beans, soaked overnight in
  cold water
6 oz prunes, covered in
  boiling water and left to
  soak overnight
1 large aubergine, cut into
  1 inch cubes

1 large onion, sliced
2 cloves garlic, crushed
1 tablespoon vegetable oil
1 vegetable stock cube
4 carrots, sliced
1 tablespoon tomato purée
1 teaspoon basil
1 tablespoon parsley
¼ pint red wine
Sea salt and black pepper

Drain soaked beans, then cover in plenty of fresh salted water, bring to the boil and simmer for about 1 hour until just tender. Drain, reserving the cooking water.
Meanwhile, cover aubergine pieces in salt, leave for 30 minutes or

so to allow bitter juices to drain away, then rinse in cold water. Drain prunes and remove stones.

Sauté onion and garlic in oil. Add cooked beans together with ½ pint of the reserved water they were cooked in, vegetable stock cube, tomato purée, herbs and black pepper, aubergine, carrots, prunes and the red wine. Bring to the boil then cover pan and simmer, stirring occasionally, for 30 minutes.

Serve with crusty wholemeal bread or on *Brown Rice\**, and supply a green salad.

Alternatively, use Beans and Aubergine in Wine to make a *Bean and Aubergine Lasagne\**.

---

## SOYA BEAN SAVOURY

6 oz soya beans, soaked overnight and cooked in the same water for about 3 hours until soft
1 large carrot, grated
1 large onion, finely chopped
1 tablespoon vegetable oil

1 tablespoon soya sauce
1 tablespoon tomato purée
2 eggs, beaten in ¼ pint yoghurt or milk
½ teaspoon each of marjoram and basil
Black pepper

Mash the drained soya beans.

Cook the carrot and onion in the vegetable oil and soya sauce until soft. Add the mashed soya beans and the remainder of the ingredients. Mix well.

Put into a greased oven dish, top with sliced tomatoes and bake at No.5, 375°F, for about 45 minutes until firm.

Serve with a side salad or green vegetables and boiled or baked potatoes.

*Variation*

Add 4 oz grated cheese to the mixture OR 4 oz chopped nuts — walnuts, peanuts or almonds.

**Soya-bean Loaf**

Add 4 oz rolled oats or wholemeal breadcrumbs to any of the above recipes. Pack into a well greased loaf tin and bake as before. When cooked turn out and garnish with parsley, tomatoes, nuts, etc to taste. Serve hot with a sauce, or slice cold and eat with a salad.

## LENTIL AND NUT RISSOLES

4 oz brown lentils, washed
  and soaked overnight in
  cold water
1 large onion, finely chopped
1 clove garlic, crushed
1 vegetable stock cube
2 oz wholemeal breadcrumbs
3 oz ground nuts

1 tablespoon parsley
1 teaspoon yeast extract
1 apple, grated
1 egg, beaten
Sea salt and black pepper
Wholemeal flour and
  vegetable oil to cook

Put soaked lentils in a pan with just enough of the water they were soaked in to just cover. Add chopped onion, crushed garlic, vegetable stock cube and a little salt. Bring to the boil, and simmer covered for about 30 minutes or until lentils are tender. Drain well. Put breadcrumbs, nuts, parsley and some pepper in a bowl, then add drained lentils, yeast extract, grated apple and egg. Mix well. Form the mixture into rissoles, roll these in flour and fry gently in oil until golden brown and hot.
Serve immediately with salad or cooked vegetables. The rissoles can be served with a *White** or *Cheese Sauce** if preferred.

## NUT LOAF

2 onions, finely chopped
2 tablespoons vegetable oil
2 tomatoes, skinned and
  chopped
2 eating apples, finely
  chopped or grated
1 teaspoon yeast extract
8 oz ground mixed nuts —
  peanuts, cashews, walnuts,
  almonds, hazelnuts

1 teaspoon caraway seeds,
  ground with nuts
1 tablespoon chopped parsley
½ teaspoon each marjoram
  and sage
2 eggs
3 Weetabix cereal biscuits
  OR 2 oz wholemeal
  breadcrumbs
Sea salt and pepper

Sauté onions in oil until tender. Add tomatoes, apples and yeast extract, and stir while cooking for 2 minutes.
Remove from heat and add ground nuts and caraway seeds, herbs, Weetabix or breadcrumbs, and eggs to make mixture fairly moist. Season with salt and pepper.

Grease a loaf tin and line the base with greaseproof paper, which should then be well oiled to prevent loaf from sticking.
Pile nut mixture into the tin and cover with foil.
Bake at No.4, 350°F, for about 1½ hours or longer, until firm.
Turn out and slice to serve.

*Nut loaf can be served hot or cold, accompanied with cranberry jelly or a sweet pickle, and makes an ideal alternative to roast meat. Lovely with a White Sauce\*.*

---

## PEANUT AND SUNFLOWER SEED PUDDING

1 large onion, finely chopped
1 green pepper, finely chopped
1 clove garlic, crushed (optional)
2 tablespoons vegetable oil
3 oz peanuts, chopped
1 teaspoon yeast extract
1 teaspoon coriander
1 tablespoon parsley
1 teaspoon thyme
Sea salt and black pepper
1 large eating apple
3 oz sunflower seeds, ground
2 oz rolled oats
½ pint milk
2 eggs

Sauté onion, pepper and garlic in oil until softened, then add peanuts and cook briefly until beginning to brown. Add coriander and yeast extract and stir over a low heat for 2 minutes.
Remove from the stove, and add parsley, thyme, salt and pepper, grated apple, ground sunflower seeds and oats. Beat egg into milk, then pour over other ingredients. Mix well, transfer to a greased pie dish, and leave to stand for 10 minutes if possible.
Cook for 1 hour at No.4, 350°F, until firm and golden.
Serve with a side salad.

---

## CHEESE AND NUT BAKE

4 oz brown rice, cooked until
  tender in about ¾ pint
  water with 1 tablespoon
  soya sauce (see
  page 116)
1 onion, finely chopped or
  grated
4 sticks celery, finely chopped
2 tablespoons vegetable oil

4 oz mixed nuts, ground or
  finely chopped
1 teaspoon mixed herbs
8 oz *Curd Cheese** or Cottage
  Cheese
2 eggs
2 oz grated cheese
Sea salt and black pepper

Sauté onion and celery in oil until tender then remove from heat
and add rice, nuts and herbs.

Beat together *Curd Cheese** or cottage cheese and eggs until thick
and creamy. This can be done if wished in a blender. Add this to
rice and nut mixture, together with grated cheese, salt and pepper.
Mix well.

Pour into a greased shallow oven dish and bake at No.4, 350°F, for
about 1 hour.

## CHILLI CON 'CARNE'

4 oz red kidney beans or
  haricot beans, soaked
  overnight in cold water
1 large onion, sliced
1 or 2 cloves garlic, crushed
1 small green pepper, finely
  chopped
4 oz button mushrooms,
  chopped
2 tablespoons vegetable oil
¾ pint water
1 vegetable stock cube

4 oz textured vegetable
  protein mince (TVP)
1 x 15 oz tin tomatoes
2 tablespoons tomato purée
2 or 3 bay leaves
1 teaspoon oregano
½ level teaspoon chilli
  powder
½ teaspoon cumin
1 teaspoon sea salt
1 teaspoon sugar

Boil beans in the same water they were soaked in for about 1½
hours or until tender, then drain.

Sauté onion, garlic, pepper and mushrooms in oil until soft. Add
water, stock cube and TVP, bring to the boil and simmer gently

covered for 5 minutes. Stir in all the remaining ingredients, including cooked beans, and simmer for 5-10 minutes more. Check seasoning finally and remove bay leaves.

Serve with *Brown Rice*\* or wholemeal bread and a side salad.

## SHEPHERDS' PIE

2 onions, finely chopped
2 tablespoons vegetable oil
4 carrots, grated
4 oz frozen peas
1½ pints water
6 oz textured vegetable
   protein mince (TVP)
2 vegetable stock cubes
1 teaspoon yeast extract

1 tablespoon tomato purée
1 tablespoon parsley
1 level teaspoon salt
Black pepper
1 level tablespoon gravy
   powder
Approximately 1 lb mashed
   potato

Sauté onion in oil until transparent then add carrots, water, peas, TVP, stock cubes, yeast extract, tomato purée, parsley, salt and pepper. Bring to the boil stirring, then simmer gently for 10 minutes. In a cup, mix gravy powder to a thin paste with a little water, pour into the pan and stir until thickened. Transfer the mixture to a pie dish and cover with the mashed potato.

Bake in the oven at No. 5, 375°F, until bubbling hot and the potato browned.

135

## MOUSSAKA

3 large or 4 medium
  aubergines

Vegetable oil
6 oz grated cheese

**Tomato Filling**

1-2 tablespoons vegetable oil
1 large onion, peeled and
  sliced
1 clove garlic, crushed
¼ lb mushrooms, sliced
1 x 15 oz can tomatoes
2 oz wholemeal breadcrumbs
1 tablespoon tomato purée

½ teaspoon yeast extract
2 oz pine nuts or sliced
  almonds (optional)
½ teaspoon each basil and
  oregano
1 teaspoon honey
Sea salt and black pepper
1 tablespoon chopped parsley

**White Sauce**

1 heaped tablespoon
  wholemeal flour

¾ pint milk

*Prepare aubergine* Slice into ¼ inch slices. Sprinkle with salt and leave for about 30 minutes, then rinse well with cold water in a colander, and drain. Fry aubergine slices lightly in a little vegetable oil until tender, then dry on absorbent paper. Put half the aubergine slices in the bottom of a greased oven dish.

*Make tomato filling* Sauté onion, garlic and mushrooms in vegetable oil until tender. Add tomatoes, breadcrumbs, tomato purée, yeast extract, nuts, herbs, honey and seasoning. Mix well. Pour tomato filling over the aubergines. Cover with half the grated cheese, and place remainder of aubergine slices to cover cheese.

*Make white sauce* Mix the flour with a little of the milk until smooth, then slowly stir in the rest of the milk. Bring to the boil stirring over a low heat until thick. (This way of making the white sauce reduces the amount of oil in the recipe.) Pour the white sauce over the aubergines, sprinkle the rest of the cheese on top, and bake in a hot oven No.4, 350°F, for 30-40 minutes until cheese topping is golden and sauce is bubbling. Serve with a green salad or vegetables.

*Variations*

Courgettes or marrow can be used instead of or as well as aubergine, but there is no need to soak either in salt.

Trim courgettes and cut into ¼ inch slices, and peel marrow and cut in half lengthwise, hollowing out centres to remove seeds. Slice thinly. Sauté the slices of either vegetable in oil until tender. Another version of this dish can be made using or including potato, which should be precooked by boiling and does not need to be fried before using in the recipe.

---

## VEGETABLES AND TOMATO AU GRATIN

Prepare and lightly cook any or a mixture of the following vegetables (see section on *Vegetables* for cooking methods).

Aubergine (slice or cut into cubes, sprinkle with salt and leave for 30 minutes. Rinse with cold water and drain, then sauté lightly in vegetable oil)
Courgettes or marrow
Leeks

Button mushrooms
Potatoes (boil and slice)
Prepare an *Italian Tomato Sauce**
4 oz grated cheese
4 oz wholemeal breadcrumbs

Place cooked vegetables in a shallow greased oven dish and cover with hot *Italian Tomato Sauce**. Mix grated cheese with breadcrumbs and sprinkle this over the top. Dot with vegetable margarine and brown under the grill. Serve immediately with a green salad.

---

## VEGETABLE MORNAY

Cover with 1 pint of *Cheese Sauce** any or a mixture of the following vegetables, lightly cooked:
Cauliflower, leeks, courgettes or marrow, onions and peppers (sliced and sautéd in vegetable oil), mushrooms, aubergine (prepared as in previous recipe) or asparagus.
Brown under the grill before serving.
  *A quick savoury classic.*

---

## RATATOUILLE

1 large aubergine, diced
1 green pepper, seeded and
  sliced
2 onions, peeled and sliced
1 or 2 cloves garlic, crushed
½ lb courgettes, sliced
2 tablespoons olive oil
1 x 8 oz can tomatoes OR

4 tomatoes skinned, and a
  dash of red wine (optional)
2 tablespoons tomato purée
1 teaspoon each oregano and
  basil
1 tablespoon chopped parsley
2 bay leaves
Sea salt and black pepper

Sprinkle aubergine cubes with salt and leave for about 30 minutes.
Rinse with cold water and drain well.

Heat oil in a large pan and add onions, peppers, garlic, drained
aubergine, and courgettes. Cook vegetables gently, stirring until
beginning to soften.

Add tomatoes, tomato purée, herbs and seasoning. Bring to the
boil, cover pan, and simmer very slowly for about 15 minutes, or
until vegetables are tender.

Remove bay leaves before serving.

*An excellent dish, Ratatouille makes an ideal starter, vegetable side
dish, or main meal, and can be eaten hot or cold. Serve hot with
grated cheese or warmed yoghurt, and accompany with wholemeal
bread, buttered noodles or baked potatoes. Serve cold as a salad with
olives or pine nuts to garnish.*

*The lovely thing about Ratatouille is that it doesn't really matter if
one or more of the vegetables has to be left out. Others that may be
more readily to hand such as celery, mushrooms and green beans, can
be used instead. Or throw them in anyway to add extra flavour – the
result is always quite delicious!*

## AUBERGINE AND CHEESE BAKE

2 large aubergines, cubed
1 large onion, peeled and
  finely chopped
2 cloves garlic, crushed
1 tablespoon vegetable oil
4 oz wholemeal bread, cut
  into small cubes

¼ pint milk
6 oz strong Cheddar cheese
1 heaped tablespoon grated
  Parmesan cheese
2 tablespoons chopped fresh
  parsley, or 1 tablespoon
  dried

2 eggs, beaten                   Sea salt and black pepper

*To garnish:*  2-4 tomatoes,
          cut into slices      (optional)

Cover the aubergines with boiling salted water and cook for about 10 minutes until tender. Drain and mash aubergines.
Heat milk and add to beaten egg. Pour over bread and allow to stand for a few minutes. Mix well.
Sauté onion and garlic in oil until soft.
Remove from heat and add aubergines, egg/bread/milk mixture, cheeses, parsley, salt and pepper.
Grease a large shallow oven dish, and spoon mixture into this. Top with tomato slices if using, and bake for about 45 minutes at No.4, 350°F, until firm and golden.
Cut into portions and serve with vegetables or a side salad.

---

## AUBERGINE AND TOMATO CRUMBLE

2 large aubergines, sliced into ¼ inch slices
2 large onions, peeled and thinly sliced
1 tablespoon olive oil
4 tomatoes
2 tablespoons tomato purée
4 tablespoons stock or wine
1 teaspoon honey
Sea salt and black pepper
1 tablespoon chopped parsley
½ teaspoon each, rosemary and thyme
4oz wholemeal breadcrumbs
4oz ground mixed nuts — hazelnuts, peanuts, sunflower seeds
2oz vegetable margarine
2 cloves garlic, crushed

Cover aubergine slices with boiling salted water and simmer for 2-3 minutes to remove bitter juices. Drain.
Sauté onion slices in oil until just tender.
Blanch tomatoes in boiling water. Drain, remove skins and slice thinly.
In a greased oven dish, put layers of onion, aubergine and tomato slices. Sprinkle with salt, pepper and herbs.
Mix together tomato purée, stock or wine, and honey, and spread over vegetables.
Combine nuts and breadcrumbs and rub in margarine. Add crushed garlic and mix well.

Spread this mixture evenly over the top of the vegetables and tomato purée and press down lightly.

Bake in the centre of the oven at No.4, 350°F, for 1 hour.

## COURGETTES BAKED WITH YOGHURT AND CHEESE

1 large onion, peeled and finely sliced
1 clove garlic, crushed
1 lb courgettes (about 3 large), washed, trimmed and cut into ¼ inch slices OR use 1 lb prepared marrow, thinly sliced
2 tablespoons vegetable oil

2 large tomatoes, sliced
1 teaspoon each basil and oregano
1 tablespoon chopped parsley
Sea salt and black pepper
⅓ pint approximately yoghurt
2 eggs, beaten
4 oz grated cheese

Sauté onion, garlic and courgette or marrow slices briefly in oil for 3 to 5 minutes. Transfer to a shallow oven dish, top with sliced tomatoes, and sprinkle with sea salt and black pepper.

Mix together eggs, yoghurt and cheese, add parsley, basil and oregano, and pour mixture over courgettes.

Bake at No.6, 400°F, for 20 to 30 minutes, or until top is set and golden. Serve with a side salad.

## AUBERGINE BAKED WITH YOGHURT AND CHEESE

Cooked in the same way as *Courgettes Baked with Yoghurt and Cheese**, using 2 medium aubergines instead of courgettes.

Cut aubergines into ¼ inch thick slices, sprinkle with salt, and leave for 30 minutes. Then rinse well with cold water and drain. Sauté with the onions and garlic, and proceed as in above recipe.

## VEGETABLES IN SOUR CREAM SAUCE WITH CRISPY TOPPING

¾ lb any of the following vegetables:
Green beans
Cauliflower florettes
Whole trimmed leeks

Whole button mushrooms
Potatoes

## Sour Cream Sauce

1 onion, finely sliced
1 green or red pepper, seeded cored and finely sliced
1 tablespoon vegetable oil
¼ pint water, stock from vegetable cooking, or white wine
1 tablespoon tomato purée
1 tablespoon chopped parsley
Pinch each, marjoram and thyme
Sea salt and pepper
¼ pint sour cream

## Crispy Topping

3 oz wholemeal breadcrumbs
2 oz sunflower seeds, ground
1 oz sesame seeds
1-2 cloves garlic, crushed
Sea salt and ground pepper
2 oz vegetable margarine
1 level tablespoon paprika

Prepare crispy topping by mixing breadcrumbs, sunflower and sesame seeds in a bowl with crushed garlic and seasoning. Melt margarine, mix with paprika, then pour onto breadcrumb mixture and mix well. Set to one side.

Quick-simmer beans, cauliflower or leeks, sauté mushrooms, or boil potatoes until tender. Reserve any cooking water to use as stock.

Prepare sauce by sautéing onion and pepper slices in the oil until tender, then add about ¼ pint of water, vegetable stock or wine. Add herbs, tomato purée and seasoning, and simmer for a few minutes. Remove from heat and stir in sour cream.

Place vegetables in a large shallow heatproof dish. Cover with sour cream sauce and top with the prepared breadcrumb mixture.

Heat under a hot grill until sauce is sizzling and the topping crispy.

*This is a lovely dish made with any of the suggested vegetables, and is also a good way of using up any left-over vegetables or potatoes. Another tasty variation is to use halved hard boiled eggs in the recipe instead of vegetables.*

## AUBERGINE AND CHEESE CASSEROLE

2 medium aubergines, thinly sliced
4 large onions, thinly sliced
1-2 cloves garlic, crushed
2 tablespoons olive oil
4 large tomatoes

1 teaspoon each, basil and oregano
2 tablespoons tomato purée
1 teaspoon honey
6-8 oz cheese, thinly sliced

Place aubergine slices in just enough boiling salted water to cover, and simmer for only 2-3 minutes to remove bitter juices quickly. Drain.
Sauté onion and garlic in oil until tender.
Blanch tomatoes in boiling water to remove skins, then chop finely. Mix tomato flesh with tomato purée, herbs and honey.
In a greased casserole dish place layers of onion and garlic, aubergine slices, tomato mixture and cheese slices, finishing with a layer of cheese.
Bake at No.5, 375°F, for 30-40 minutes.
   Serve with baked potatoes or fresh wholemeal bread and a green salad.

## SPINACH SAVOURY AU GRATIN

1 lb fresh spinach OR 1 large packet frozen chopped or puréed spinach, thawed
1/2 lb packet frozen sweetcorn kernels
1 large onion, peeled and finely sliced
Vegetable oil
3 hard boiled eggs, chopped

OR 3-4 oz chopped roasted peanuts
1 pint *Cheese Sauce*⃰
3 oz grated cheese
3 oz wholemeal breadcrumbs
Sea salt, black pepper and 1 teaspoon mixed herbs
1-2 oz vegetable margarine

Wash and roughly chop spinach, then place in a pan with about 1 tablespoon each of vegetable oil and water. Cook covered for a few minutes, shaking pan frequently to prevent sticking. Remove from heat and liquidize with juice to purée.
If using frozen spinach, cook quickly in a little vegetable oil.
Season spinach with salt, pepper and mixed herbs.
Sauté onion in 1 tablespoon oil until transparent.

Pour frozen sweetcorn into boiling water, return to the boil, and then immediately drain.

Place spinach, sweetcorn, and onion slices into a greased shallow oven dish. Cover with chopped hard boiled egg, or chopped nuts. Pour *Cheese Sauce** over vegetables and top with the grated cheese and breadcrumbs mixed together. Dot with the margarine, and cook in a hot oven, No.7, 425°F, for about 10 minutes until top is golden and crisp.

For an alternative way of making this dish, use 1 lb leeks washed and sliced or 2 peppers seeded and thinly sliced in place of spinach. Sauté either, with onion, and then proceed as before.

## HUNGARIAN CAULIFLOWER AND POTATO BAKE

1 cauliflower, broken into
  florettes
4 large potatoes, scrubbed
4 hard boiled eggs
4-6 oz grated cheese

1 carton sour cream (if not
  available, use single or
  double cream mixed with
  the juice of ½ lemon)
Sea salt and black pepper

Boil the potatoes in their skins until tender, then cool, peel, and slice thickly.

Parboil the cauliflower by cooking in boiling water for only 2-3 minutes, depending on the size of the florettes.

In a large greased casserole dish, arrange layers of potato, cauliflower and hard boiled egg, putting on each layer a little salt, pepper, sour cream and cheese. Finish with a layer of potato sprinkled with grated cheese. Bake covered at No.6, 400°F, for 30-40 minutes or until hot and bubbling. Remove the lid for the last 10 minutes to brown the top. Serve with a side salad.

## POTATO PANCAKES

¾ lb raw potato, peeled and
  grated
1 onion, grated
1 large eating apple, grated
1 heaped tablespoon each
  soya flour, wheatgerm,
  skim milk powder

1 level teaspoon sea salt
Black pepper
1 teaspoon marjoram
1 tablespoon chopped parsley
2 eggs

Mix all ingredients together in a bowl, and allow to stand for ½ hour if possible.

Heat a little vegetable oil in a frying pan, and drop tablespoons of the potato 'batter' into the pan. Fry gently until pancakes are golden brown on both sides.

For a spicy change of flavour, omit marjoram, add 1 or 2 teaspoons garam masala and serve with yoghurt spooned over the top.

*Delicious with sweet chutney or cranberry sauce, potato pancakes make a very tasty quick meal. And they're nutritious too!*

## VEGETABLE CHOP SUEY

2 onions, sliced
1 green pepper, sliced
4 sticks celery, sliced
  diagonally
2 carrots, sliced thinly
  lengthwise
2 tablespoons vegetable oil
4 oz button mushrooms,
  sliced

6 oz bean sprouts, fresh or
  tinned (drained)
4 oz frozen whole green beans
  OR cauliflower florettes
4 oz whole blanched almonds
¾ pint water
2 tablespoons soya sauce
1 level tablespoon cornflour
1 teaspoon honey
2 teaspoons yeast extract

Prepare all the vegetables beforehand. Sauté onion, pepper, celery and carrots in oil for only a few minutes. Then add mushrooms, bean sprouts, beans or cauliflower, almonds and water. Mix together in a cup the cornflour, soya sauce and honey and stir into the vegetables until thickened. Add the yeast extract, cover and simmer the mixture for only a few minutes more. Serve immediately with *Brown Rice**.

*A lovely quick Chinese dish in which the almonds and brown rice together make up complete protein.*

*For extra nourishment and variety, make an omelette, and serve rolled up to accompany the Chop Suey\*.*

---

# Stuffed Vegetables

## TOMATO AND ONION STUFFING

3 onions, peeled and finely
   chopped
2 cloves garlic, crushed
2-3 tablespoons olive oil
¾ lb tomatoes, skinned and
   chopped
2 tablespoons tomato purée
3 oz pine nuts or almonds

Sea salt and black pepper
1 teaspoon each, basil and
   oregano
3 tablespoons fresh chopped
   parsley, or 1 tablespoon
   dried
1 teaspoon honey or sugar

Sauté onion and garlic in oil until soft. If stuffing aubergine or courgettes, sauté the removed chopped flesh with the onions and garlic (see relevant recipe method). Add tomatoes and cook stirring for a few minutes. Stir in all other ingredients.

---

## TOMATO AND NUT STUFFING

1 large onion, finely chopped
1 clove garlic, crushed
2 tablespoons vegetable oil
4 large tomatoes, skinned and
   chopped
4 oz button mushrooms,
   finely chopped (optional)
3 oz wholemeal breadcrumbs

4 oz ground mixed nuts
1 tablespoon tomato purée
½ teaspoon mixed herbs
1 tablespoon chopped parsley
Juice of ½ lemon
Sea salt and black pepper,
   to taste

**N.B.** When stuffing courgettes, the scooped out centres can be chopped and used instead of mushrooms (see recipe).

Sauté onion and garlic in oil until soft. Add tomatoes and mushrooms or courgette centres, and cook for a few minutes. Add all other ingredients, and combine well.

## CHEESE AND RICE STUFFING

4 oz brown rice
1 medium onion, finely chopped
2 cloves garlic, crushed
1 tablespoon olive oil
4 oz mushrooms, finely chopped

1 tablespoon chopped parsley
Sea salt and pepper
Dash of tabasco
1 egg, beaten
4 oz grated cheese

Wash rice well in cold water, then cook gently in a covered pan in just less than ¾ pint of boiling salted water, until water is absorbed and the rice tender. Meanwhile, sauté onion and garlic in the oil until tender. Add mushrooms and parsley and cook for a few minutes more until soft.
Add cooked rice and all other ingredients. Mix well.

## RICE AND SUNFLOWER SEED STUFFING

4 oz brown rice
Soya sauce
2 onions, finely chopped
1-2 cloves garlic, crushed
2 tablespoons vegetable oil
4 tomatoes, skinned and chopped

1 tablespoon finely chopped parsley
½ teaspoon basil
1 tablespoon tomato purée
Sea salt and black pepper
4 oz ground sunflower seeds

Wash rice well in cold water, then cook slowly in a covered pan in just less than ¾ pint of boiling water with 1 tablespoon of soya sauce added, until all the water is absorbed and the rice tender. Sauté onion and garlic in oil until soft, then add tomatoes, herbs, tomato purée, sunflower seeds and cooked rice. Mix well. Season to taste.

## WALNUT AND PARMESAN CHEESE STUFFING

1 large onion, finely chopped     1-2 cloves garlic, crushed

146

1 tablespoon olive oil
4 tomatoes, skinned and
 chopped
6 black or green olives, sliced
3 oz chopped walnuts
3 oz wholemeal breadcrumbs
3-4 tablespoons grated
 Parmesan cheese

1 egg, beaten
Juice of ½ lemon
1 tablespoon each of mint
 and dill
1 tablespoon chopped parsley
Sea salt and black pepper

Sauté onion and garlic in oil until soft. Aubergine or courgette flesh can be added at this stage if stuffing those vegetables (see recipe). Add tomatoes, and cook, stirring for a few minutes. Remove from heat and mix in all the other ingredients.

---

## AUBERGINE WITH TOMATO AND ONION STUFFING

2 medium aubergines
*Tomato and Onion Stuffing*\*
 ingredients

3-4 oz grated cheese,
 Parmesan or other type

Wipe skins and cut aubergines in half lengthwise. (They may be peeled if preferred).
Scoop out centres carefully, leaving a good ¼ inch shell. Chop scooped out flesh. Sprinkle the hollowed out shells and the chopped flesh with salt and leave for about ½ hour. Rinse shells and flesh well with cold water and drain.
Make *Tomato and Onion Stuffing*\* adding aubergine flesh to sauté with onion, garlic and tomatoes (see recipe).
Place drained aubergine shells in a greased shallow oven dish. Fill with stuffing mixture and top with grated cheese.
For a crispy topping, mix 2-3 oz wholemeal breadcrumbs with the cheese. Bake at No.4, 350°F, for about 40 minutes until aubergine shells are tender. Serve with a green salad or vegetables.

*This recipe can also be served as a starter, either hot or cold. To serve cold, cook as above but omit cheese and breadcrumbs. Cool and serve with yoghurt spooned over the top and garnish with parsley and lemon slices.*

---

## AUBERGINE WITH CHEESE AND RICE STUFFING

2 large or 4 small aubergines      *Cheese and Rice Stuffing**

Wipe the skins, then cut a slice off the stem end of the aubergines to remove hull and stem. Scoop out the inside flesh, being careful not to break the skins, and leave about ¼ inch shell. Reserve the flesh for sauce.

Sprinkle the insides of the shells with salt and leave them inverted in a colander for at least 30 minutes to allow the bitter juices to drain away. Then rinse out well with cold water.

Prepare the *Cheese and Rice Stuffing** and carefully fill each aubergine shell. Wrap the stuffed aubergine tightly in tin foil, and bake in the oven at No.4, 350°F, for about 1-1½ hours.

Prepare an *Aubergine and Tomato Sauce** using the aubergine pulp; there is no real need to salt this beforehand, but it can be done if preferred.

Serve the stuffed aubergine either one per person if they are small, or if larger cut in half lengthwise, making two portions out of each aubergine. Accompany with the sauce and a green salad or vegetable.

## AUBERGINE WITH WALNUT AND PARMESAN CHEESE STUFFING

2 large or 4 small aubergines      *Walnut and Parmesan Stuffing** ingredients

Prepare the aubergine as in *Aubergine with Cheese and Rice Stuffing**. Chop the removed aubergine flesh and use in the *Walnut and Parmesan Cheese Stuffing** (see recipe). Bake as previous recipe. Serve ½ a large or 1 small aubergine per person, and accompany with *Tomato** or *Wine Sauce** and a green salad.

## CABBAGE LEAVES WITH CHEESE AND RICE STUFFING

10-12 large young cabbage
  leaves
*Cheese and Rice Stuffing**
2-3 tablespoons tomato purée

¼ pint water
1 tablespoon vegetable oil
½ teaspoon brown sugar
1 teaspoon basil

Place the cabbage leaves into boiling salted water and cook for a few minutes to soften. Drain well.
Put about 1 tablespoon of stuffing onto each leaf, fold the sides of the leaf towards the middle and roll up.
Place securely side by side in a greased flat oven dish.
Blend the tomato purée, water, vegetable oil, sugar and basil and pour over cabbage leaves.
Cover with lid or tinfoil, and cook at No.4, 350°F, for ½-¾ hour.
Serve basted with the juice they were cooked in.

## CABBAGE LEAVES WITH WALNUT AND PARMESAN CHEESE STUFFING

Recipe as above but using *Walnut and Parmesan Cheese Stuffing**.
Leave out the basil in the basting sauce and use parsley or chives instead.

## CABBAGE LEAVES WITH RICE AND SUNFLOWER SEED STUFFING

Recipe as before but using *Rice and Sunflower Seed Stuffing**.

*A rich cheese sauce is very good served with cabbage leaves filled this way.*

## COURGETTE WITH TOMATO AND ONION STUFFING

| | |
|---|---|
| 4 large courgettes | 3-4 oz grated cheese — |
| *Tomato and Onion Stuffing** ingredients | Parmesan or other |

Trim courgettes and boil in salted water for 3 minutes. Drain, cool and cut in half lengthwise. Scoop out centres, and place courgette halves in a greased shallow oven dish.
Make *Tomato and Onion Stuffing**, adding the chopped courgette centres. Fill courgette halves with stuffing mixture and top with grated cheese.
For a more crispy topping, mix 2-3 oz wholemeal breadcrumbs with the cheese.
Bake at No.4, 350°F for about 30-40 minutes.
*A delicious light meal served with a green salad, this recipe also makes an unusual starter. For a cold salad variation, omit cheese and breadcrumbs before cooking. Then cool and serve cold with maybe some yoghurt spooned over the top. Garnish with parsley and lemon slices.*

## COURGETTES WITH TOMATO AND NUT STUFFING

4 large courgettes      *Tomato and Nut Stuffing** ingredients

Prepare and cook as above, but using *Tomato and Nut Stuffing**.
Include chopped courgette centres in stuffing recipe.
Serve with a *White** or *Cheese Sauce**, and a green salad.

## COURGETTES WITH WALNUT AND PARMESAN CHEESE STUFFING

4 large courgettes

*Walnut and Parmesan Cheese Stuffing\* ingredients*

Prepare courgettes as in previous recipe.
Make *Walnut and Parmesan Cheese Stuffing\**, adding chopped courgette flesh to sauté with onion, garlic and tomatoes.
Pile stuffing into courgette halves and bake in a shallow greased oven dish at No.4, 350°F, for 30 minutes.
Serve with a *Tomato\** or *Wine Sauce\**, and a green salad.

## MARROW WITH RICE AND SUNFLOWER SEED STUFFING

1 medium sized marrow

*Rice and Sunflower Seed Stuffing\**

Cut the ends off the marrow and scoop out the hard inside flesh and seeds with a spoon, leaving a tubular cavity. Boil marrow in salted water for 5 minutes, then drain and fill with stuffing. Wrap securely in foil and bake at No.6, 400°F for about ¾ hour or until marrow is tender.
Serve marrow cut in slices crosswise, and accompany with *Tomato or Wine Sauce\**, and a green salad.

*Variation*
Large courgettes can be prepared and filled in the same way, but scooped out flesh could be chopped and sautéd with the onions for the sauce. Serve whole.

## MARROW RINGS WITH TOMATO AND NUT STUFFING

1 medium marrow          *Tomato and Nut Stuffing**

Prepare marrow as in previous recipe and boil in salted water for 5 minutes. Drain, then cut into slices, allowing 1-2 generous sized 'rings' for each person.
Place marrow rings in a shallow, well oiled baking dish, and place spoonfuls of the stuffing into the middle of each ring.
Cover dish with foil or a lid, and bake at No.4, 350°F, for about 30 minutes until marrow rings are tender.
Garnish each stuffed ring with parsley, and serve with a *White** or *Cheese Sauce**.

## PEPPERS WITH CHEESE AND RICE STUFFING

4 green peppers          *Cheese and Rice Stuffing**

Cut and reserve a slice from the stalk end of each of the peppers to leave the top open and carefully remove pith and seeds from the insides. Boil peppers in salted water for 3 minutes, then drain. Prepare *Cheese and Rice Stuffing** and fill the peppers. Place upright and closely fitting in a well oiled oven dish, cover with a lid of tinfoil, and bake at No.4, 350°F for about 40-50 minutes. Serve with *Italian Tomato Sauce** replacing the ½ pepper in the recipe with the chopped-up reserved pepper tops, and omitting mushrooms from the sauce if you like.

## PEPPERS WITH WALNUT AND PARMESAN CHEESE STUFFING

4 green peppers          *Walnut and Parmesan Stuffing**

Prepare the peppers as in the previous recipe and fill with *Walnut and Parmesan Stuffing**. Bake as before. Serve with a *Tomato**, *Wine** or *White Sauce**.

## PEPPERS WITH RICE AND SUNFLOWER
## SEED STUFFING

4 green peppers                    *Rice and Sunflower Seed*
                                   *Stuffing**

As above, using *Rice and Sunflower Seed Stuffing**.
Serve with *Tomato** or *Wine Sauce**.

# *Snacks*

In this section I have suggested some ideas for snacks that are quick, tasty enough to keep away thoughts of the biscuit tin, and nutritious enough to serve as a hurried meal:

To fill the last requirement, some of the *Protein Salads** are very quick to prepare. Try a *Waldorf Salad** or *Cabbage, Apple and Peanut Salad**, and accompany with wholemeal bread or crispbread. Or, if you have any of the *Spreads, Pâtés or Dips** from that recipe section to hand, then these make ideal sandwich fillers, garnished with salad vegetables and followed by fresh fruit.

A perfect light meal for weight watchers, and a very tasty one too, is to prepare a fresh fruit salad of maybe banana, apple and pear, or half an avocado. Top with cottage cheese and serve on a bed of lettuce or cress. Or mix either mashed banana or grated apple with yoghurt. Add a little honey if you like.

Other very good yoghurt based snack meals could include *Fruit and Yoghurt Breakfast** or yoghurt combined with *Wheatgerm and Nut Mix**. And there are more yoghurt ideas on page 161.

Then there's always the classic *Ploughman's Lunch*! With wholemeal bread or crispbread, serve a good hunk of cheese (otherwise cottage cheese or a hard boiled egg are just as good) and some pickle if you have any. Surround with a salad garnish such as tomato, onion and pepper slices, lettuce, cress, raw carrot, and any other favourite raw vegetable available. And if you've any soup made up, a bowlful could be a welcome addition.

As an alternative to the Ploughman's, spread wholemeal bread or crispbread with peanut butter, and top with cheese, cottage cheese, banana or pineapple.

Try a handful of mixed nuts, seeds and raisins followed by a yoghurt or fresh fruit for excellent nourishment.

If what is wanted is a warming, quickly prepared meal, then the following hot snack ideas might be helpful. Serve them with a salad garnish or a side salad from the salad section:

Spread peanut butter generously onto hot buttered wholemeal toast, and top with grilled tomato halves. This is really quite delicious and a great favourite with my children!

Onto wholemeal toast, place slices of cheese and melt under a hot grill until golden and bubbling. (Remember cheese-on-toast?)

Make cheese sandwiches with wholemeal bread. Soak these in beaten egg and fry on both sides in a little vegetable oil until golden brown. Serve with sweet pickle.

With a bit more time in hand, nothing could be easier than making *Savoury Stuffed Pancakes** and filling them with any of the quick protein suggestions on page 107.

Or if you're near the oven an hour or two before a quick meal is needed, scrub some medium or large sized potatoes, wrap them in foil and put them in the oven at No.4, 350°F, for 1-2 hours, depending on their size. But the joy of baked potatoes is that there are no hard and fast rules about cooking them. The oven can be turned down low and the potatoes left in there all morning if necessary. Then just before serving, unwrap the foil, make a deep slit in each potato, opening them up slightly, and fill with grated cheese. Return to the oven briefly or put under a hot grill to melt and brown the cheese, and serve with a salad garnish.

# *Puddings, Cakes, Biscuits and Bread*

By far the most favourable puddings, between-meal snacks or sandwich-box fillers are fresh and dried fruits. These contain a wealth of natural health-giving nutrients, and there is always a plentiful selection available throughout the year.

With a little careful thought, puddings can also serve to contribute to the nutritional value of a meal. For example, by providing yoghurt or cheese for dessert, protein content is considerably increased.

However, old habits die hard, and there are those special occasions when thoughts of more conventional puddings, cakes or biscuits may be hard to ignore! For those times, the recipes in this section make full use of whole foods while keeping sugar content minimal. Honey, being the healthiest sweetening agent, is used whenever possible, and sometimes raw cane sugar in moderate amounts. And while the over-sweet, synthetic puddings and confectionary products too frequently consumed today are full of empty calories and health damaging ingredients, the following recipes provide tasty alternatives which also contain some nutritional goodness.

159

Also in this section are easy 'real' bread recipes to provide vital nourishment with the unbeatable taste (and smell!) of freshly baked wholemeal bread.

## WAYS WITH FRUIT

Fruits, like vegetables, are healthier eaten raw, and colourful interesting combinations of fresh or dried fruit make a perfect pudding every time!

To enjoy fresh fruit at its best soft perishable fruits ought to be eaten within 24 hours while hard skinned fruits will keep for several days. And a fresh fruit salad ideally should be prepared only shortly before needed; over-exposure to air and light will result in a rapid loss of vitamins and minerals. Retain the skins of such fruits as apples, pears, peaches and apricots as these provide vital roughage and nutrients. Chop up any available fresh fruits, toss in lemon juice to prevent them from going brown too quickly, and trickle a little honey over to sweeten if necessary. If the fruit salad is not to be served immediately, cover well and place in the fridge or a cool place. Serve with honey sweetened yoghurt.

For a dried fruit salad, cover a selection of mixed dried fruits with boiling water, add some honey and a little molasses, then leave to soak overnight. This method of preparing dried fruit means that they become tender without having to be cooked (see also page 30).

---

## FRUIT PURÉES

### Apple

½-2lbs cooking apples,
  peeled, cored and sliced

Place apples in a pan with at least ¼ pint water or enough to just cover the bottom. Stew gently until soft, then purée apples along with the juice in a blender, through a seive or food mill, or mash with a wooden spoon. Add finally 1-2 tablespoons honey or raw cane sugar to sweeten.

**N.B.** If you have a food mill there is no real need to peel and core the apples. Just chop and cook as above, then when soft pass through the mill. This method possibly retains a greater quantity of nutrients.

## Apricot or Prune

8 oz dried apricots or prunes
   (a mixture is also very good)

Just cover dried fruit with boiling water. Stir in 1 tablespoon
honey and 1 teaspoon molasses. Leave to soak overnight or longer.
When fruits are soft, remove stones from prunes, and purée either
fruit in a blender with enough of the water they were soaked in to
make this easy.

*These fruit purées are delicious on their own and topped with
yoghurt. Or they can form a basis for other puddings, such as Rice and
Fruit Dessert\*, Wholewheat Pancakes\*, and Fruit Purée Yoghurt\*.*

**N.B.**   For information on correct food combining with fruits,
         refer to pages 36-40.

---

## PUDDINGS WITH YOGHURT

To sweeten yoghurt, add about 1 teaspoon honey to each ¼ pint
(1 carton) yoghurt and eat on its own or blended to any of the
following varieties.
Quantities given to mix with approximately ¼ pint (1 carton)
yoghurt, are sufficient for 1-2 people.

**Nut and Raisin Yoghurt** Use 1 heaped tablespoon each of
hazelnuts and raisins to every ¼ pint yoghurt
Pour a little boiling water over raisins to plump up, and leave for
several hours. Coarsely grind or chop the nuts, then drain the
raisins and add the nuts to the honey-sweetened yoghurt.

**Muesli Yoghurt**
Finely grind 1 heaped tablespoon of *Ready to Eat Muesli\** for each
¼ pint of honey sweetened yoghurt. Mix well.

**Banana Yoghurt**
Take 1 banana for every ¼ pint yoghurt. Mash well and mix with
honey-sweetened yoghurt.

**Fruit Purée Yoghurt**
Mix equal quantities of *Fruit Purée\** and yoghurt. Add honey to
taste if required.

**Strawberry Yoghurt**
Mash 2-4 oz strawberries and mix with ¼ pint honey-sweetened yoghurt.

---

## CREAMY RICE AND APRICOT DESSERT

1 cup of cooked *Brown Rice*\* (about 3 oz uncooked)
1 cup plain yoghurt (about 2 cartons)

1 cup *Apricot Purée*\* (made (from about 4 oz dried apricots).
2 oz almonds, ground
1 level tablespoon thin honey

Mix all ingredients together well, chill slightly and spoon into glasses to serve.

---

## APPLE CHEESE CAKE

**Biscuit Base**
4 oz wholemeal flour
1 oz wheatgerm

1-2 tablespoons raw cane sugar
3 oz vegetable margarine

**Filling**
2 eating apples, peeled and cored
8 oz *Curd Cheese*\*

2 tablespoons honey
1 egg
¼ pint yoghurt or thin cream

Make biscuit base by mixing flour, wheatgerm and brown sugar together, then rub in vegetable margarine. Press this into a greased flan dish. Slice apples thinly and arrange in circles overlapping slightly, on the biscuit base.
Beat or blend the remaining ingredients together until thick and creamy, then pour over the apples.
Bake for about 40 minutes at No.3, 325°F, until firm.
Cool and serve chilled.

*Variation*
Omit the apple from the recipe and cook as above. When cool, cover the cheese cake with soft fruits in season, such as strawberries or raspberries. These fruits can be lightly tossed in a lemon and honey mixture beforehand to sweeten and preserve them.

---

## APPLE CRUMBLE

About 1 lb cooking apples
2 tablespoons honey
 according to taste
Pinch of allspice (optional)
Dash lemon juice or orange
 juice

3 oz rolled oats
3 oz wholemeal breadcrumbs
2 oz raw cane sugar
3 oz vegetable margarine
The grated peel of 1 lemon
 or orange

Peel and finely slice apples. Place in a well greased pie dish and trickle honey and fruit juice over.

Combine the oats, breadcrumbs and sugar. Melt the margarine and pour this over the mixture, together with the grated peel of lemon or orange. Mix up well.

Spread crumb mixture over apples, and bake at No.4, 350°F, for about 45 minutes until apples are soft and crumble golden brown.

*Other fruit can be used to make a crumble. Try plums or soft fruits such as strawberries and blackcurrants, or dried apricots or other dried fruits that have been well soaked before cooking.*

## BANANAS FLAMBÉ

4 bananas
4 tablespoons maple syrup

4 tablespoons brandy

In a greased flat serving dish, place the peeled whole bananas, and trickle over the maple syrup. Cover with lid or tin foil, and put in a hot oven for 5-10 minutes to just heat through.
Warm the brandy in a small pan, then at the table pour this over the bananas and flame with a match.
Serve immediately.

## ALMOND STUFFED PRUNES

½ lb prunes
Boiling water
Whole almonds
2 tablespoons maple syrup or
　honey

Dash of lemon juice
2 tablespoons brandy or
　other liqueur (optional)

**N.B.** If using liqueur, decrease the liquid used when cooking stuffed prunes by 2 tablespoons.

Place prunes in a basin, pour boiling water over them to cover, and leave to soak overnight or longer until swollen and soft.
Drain, reserving liquid, and carefully remove stones through one end with a small sharp knife. This is easier than it sounds if the prunes have had a good long soak. But if you do find it hard, bring the prunes to the boil in their liquid, and cook for 5 minutes or so until they are more tender. Then drain, reserving liquid as before, cool and stone.
Replace stones with an almond in each prune.
Place stuffed prunes in a pan with ¼ pint of the reserved liquid in which they were soaked or cooked, together with syrup or honey, and brandy or other liqueur if using. Cover pan and simmer very gently for about ½ hour, during which time the syrup will be absorbed by the nuts and prunes. If this happens too quickly add a dash more of the reserved prune liquid, but this should not be necessary if they are simmering on a low enough heat.
Transfer to a shallow serving dish, cool, and serve chilled, garnished with twists of orange or lemon, and with an accompanying bowl of honey-sweetened yoghurt or cream.
　*With or without liqueur, this is a most exquisite pudding and will finish off any meal in style.*

## PANCAKES

Make pancakes using the basic batter mixture (with all milk) and method given for *Wholemeal Pancakes** on page 106, and fill with any of the following suggestions to make delicious and always popular puddings.

Serve piping hot: Pancakes filled with a *Fruit Purée**.

Pancakes filled with finely chopped nuts such as hazelnuts, walnuts or almonds. Trickle a little honey or maple syrup over the nuts before rolling up.

Pancakes filled with lemon juice and a little honey or maple syrup.

## CRÊPES SUZETTES

Make *Wholemeal Pancakes** and while still hot in the pan sprinkle each one with a little raw cane sugar and lemon juice. Fold into four and place pancakes in a greased oven-to-table dish. Keep warm in the oven. Make a sauce by mixing together 4 tablespoons orange juice and 2 tablespoons honey or maple syrup. Heat through and pour over the pancakes. Just before serving, warm about 2 tablespoons brandy, pour over the pancakes and sauce, flame and bring to the table alight.

## SEMOLINA PUDDING

2oz wholewheat semolina      1 pint milk
1-2 tablespoons honey

Bring the milk nearly to boiling point, then sprinkle on the semolina, stirring all the time until thick. Reduce heat to very minimum and cook, stirring regularly to prevent burning, for about 10 minutes. Add honey finally.

## BAKED EGG CUSTARD

4 eggs      1 pint warmed milk
2 tablespoons honey

Beat eggs and honey together. Pour the warmed milk over the mixture, then empty into a greased pie dish. Stand the dish in a container of cold water and bake at No.1, 275°F, until firm; about 1½ hours.

## BREAD PUDDING

2 large or 4 small slices of
  wholemeal bread (about
  4 oz)
2 oz raisins
2 eggs, beaten

1 pint milk
2 tablespoons honey
1 oz vegetable margarine
Nutmeg

Cut the slices of bread into large squares and lay these in a greased shallow baking dish. Sprinkle with raisins. Heat the milk, together with margarine and honey, until these are dissolved. Add the beaten eggs and whisk lightly with a fork to mix, then pour onto the bread and leave to stand for 30 minutes. Sprinkle with a little nutmeg and bake at No.3, 325°F, for about 1 hour or until set.

## QUICK WHOLEMEAL BREAD

For one loaf:
1 lb wholemeal flour
1 teaspoon sea salt
3 teaspoons dried yeast

1 teaspoon raw cane sugar
$\frac{1}{2}$ pint warm water
1 teaspoon vegetable oil

Place about 3 fluid oz of the warm water in a bowl and sprinkle in the yeast and sugar. Beat with a fork until dissolved, then leave in a warm place until frothy (about 10 minutes). Mix the flour and salt together, and add the yeast mixture together with the rest of the water and the oil. Stir until the mixture forms a dough, then turn on to a lightly floured surface and knead well for 5 minutes. Shape the dough to fit snugly inside a greased 2 lb bread tin. Place the tin inside a polythene bag or cover with a clean cloth, and leave in a warm place to rise until the dough is doubled in size and about 1 inch over the top of the tin (about 45 minutes).
Bake at No.6, 400°F, for about 45 minutes. To test if the loaf is cooked, when removed from the tin it should sound hollow when tapped.
  *Bread is made primarily with wheat flour because wheat contains more gluten than any other grain. Gluten is the substance, developed by kneading, that makes the dough stretch and enables it to form bread. But to vary or enrich the Quick Wholemeal Bread recipe, substitute 4 oz of the wholemeal flour with 2 oz of other flours – barley, rye or millet. Or use soya flour, wheatgerm, oatmeal or*

*cracked wheat. Make up the full quantity of flour with 2 oz* unbleached strong white *flour. This contains more gluten than wholemeal flour, so will compensate for the less glutinous properties of the other ingredients and result in lighter bread.*

*If you have any porridge or cooked grain left over, these will also enhance the taste and quality of wholemeal bread. Add about ½ cup of cooked (cooled) porridge or grain to the Quick Wholemeal Bread recipe by working it in after kneading the dough.*

## SOFT BROWN ROLLS

10 oz wholemeal flour
4 oz strong white flour
2 oz wheatgerm
1 teaspoon sea salt
3 tablespoons dried yeast
3 teaspoons raw cane sugar

1 tablespoon vegetable oil
7 fluid oz warm water
1 heaped tablespoon skim
  milk powder
1 egg, beaten

Sprinkle the yeast and sugar into about half the warm water. Beat with a fork until dissolved, then leave in a warm place to froth (about 10 minutes). Mix the flours, wheatgerm and salt in a bowl. Stir the milk powder into the rest of the water and pour onto the flour, together with the yeast mixture, the oil and the beaten egg. Stir well to make the dough. Turn out and knead on a lightly floured board for 5 minutes, then return the dough to the basin, cover with a cloth and leave in a warm place for about 45 minutes or until doubled in size. Turn out again and knead briefly to knock out the air bubbles. Divide the dough into 8-10 equal pieces, then roll each lightly into a round or long shape. Space these out on a greased baking tray, cover with a cloth and leave in a warm place to double in size (about 15 minutes).

Remove the cloth and bake at No.6, 400°F, for 10-15 minutes.

*Variation*

**Fresh-for-Breakfast Rolls**

Prepare the bread dough as above during the early evening. But after the once risen dough has been divided into roll shapes and placed on a baking tray, put the tin inside a large polythene bag, and store in the fridge overnight (6-8 hours) to double in size more slowly. In the morning, prepare the oven early, and bake the rolls as before. Allow to cool slightly before serving.

## WHOLEMEAL SCONES

8 oz wholemeal flour  
Good pinch sea salt  
4 level teaspoons baking powder

2 oz vegetable margarine  
¼ pint milk

Mix flour, salt and baking powder in a bowl. Rub in the margarine, then stir in the milk and mix to a soft dough.
Roll out on a floured board to about ¾ inch thickness and cut into rounds. Bake on a greased baking tray for 10-15 minutes at No.8, 450°F.

## OATMEAL WAFERS

4 oz oatmeal  
4 oz wholemeal flour  
1 teaspoon baking powder  
½ teaspoon sea salt

2 oz vegetable margarine  
1 level teaspoon molasses  
A little milk

Mix oatmeal, flour, baking powder and salt. Rub in the margarine and molasses, then add just enough milk to form mixture into a stiff dough. Roll out thinly on a floured board, cut into rounds, and bake on an oven tray for 20-30 minutes at No.4, 350°F, or until firm and golden. Cool on a wire rack. Serve buttered, with honey or cheese.

## CHEESE STRAWS

8 oz wholemeal flour  
4 oz vegetable margarine  
4 oz grated Cheddar cheese

1 egg, beaten  
A little milk or water to bind

Rub the margarine well into the flour. Add the grated cheese and most of the beaten egg (reserving a bit for glazing). Mix together, then add a very little amount of water or milk if necessary to bind. Roll out dough to about ¼ inch thick, and cut into long thin slices. Carefully place on a greased oven tray and brush with the reserved beaten egg.
Bake at No.7, 450°F, for approximately 10-15 minutes until golden. Cool on the tin for a few minutes, then remove onto a cooling tray with a palette knife.

## MUESLI BISCUITS

8 oz *Ready to Eat Muesli*\*
2 tablespoons wholemeal
   flour
3 oz vegetable margarine

2 tablespoons dark raw cane
   sugar
1 heaped tablespoon honey
2 tablespoons water

Combine Muesli and flour in a bowl. Melt margarine, honey and sugar in a pan, then add to the Muesli, with the water. Mix all together well. Press mixture into a greased swiss roll tin or baking tray and bake at No.3, 325°F, for 20-30 minutes until golden and crisp. Leave in the tin to cool slightly before marking into squares, then remove when cold.

## SESAME AND PEANUT BUTTER BISCUITS

2 heaped tablespoons Tahini
   (sesame paste)
2 heaped tablespoons peanut
   butter
3 heaped tablespoons honey

1 egg
2 oz wholemeal flour
½ level teaspoon baking
   powder
Walnut halves

Beat together Tahini, peanut butter, honey and egg. Add the flour and baking powder and mix well. Place spoonfuls of the mixture onto a greased baking tray and put a walnut half in the centre of each biscuit.
Bake at No.4, 350°F, for 15-20 minutes. Allow the biscuits to cool slightly before removing them from the tin onto a cooling tray.

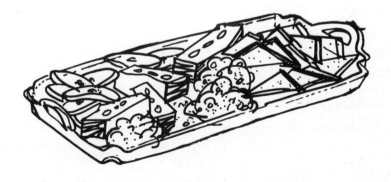

## BRAN LOAF

3 oz bran
1 oz wheatgerm
½ pint milk
1 teaspoon molasses
4-5 tablespoons thin honey

2 oz ground mixed nuts
2 oz chopped dates or raisins
4 oz self raising 85%
   wholemeal flour

Mix the bran, wheatgerm, milk, molasses and honey, and leave to stand for at least 1 hour. Then stir in all the other ingredients and transfer the mixture into a well greased loaf tin. Bake in the oven at No.4 350°F, for about 1-1½ hours until firm. Turn out of the tin and cool on a wire tray. Serve sliced and buttered.

## HONEY WHOLEMEAL SPONGE CAKE

4 oz vegetable margarine
3 tablespoons thin honey
2 eggs

6 oz wholemeal flour
1 teaspoon baking powder

Cream the margarine and honey together until pale and creamy. Beat in the eggs, one at a time, then fold in the flour and and baking powder.
Divide the mixture between two greased and lined 7 inch sandwich cake tins and bake at No.4, 350°F, for 20-25 minutes, until firm to touch and golden. Turn out onto a wire cooking tray and when cool sandwich with a low sugar marmalade or jam.

*Variations*

**Chocolate Sponge Cake**
As above, but add 1 tablespoon carob powder with the flour.

**Hazelnut Torte**
Use only 3 oz wholemeal flour together with 3 oz finely ground hazelnuts. Fill with a low sugar jam.

## HONEY, FRUIT AND NUT CAKE

6 oz vegetable margarine
3 very full tablespoons thin
  honey
3 eggs, beaten
8 oz wholewheat flour
2 oz wheatgerm
2 heaped teaspoons baking
  powder
1 lb fruit, incorporating some
  or all of the following:
  Sultanas, raisins or currants
  Mashed banana
Chopped dates
Chopped pineapple
Dried prunes or apricots,
  presoaked and chopped
3 oz hazelnuts, ground or
  finely chopped
3 oz sunflower seeds, ground
Rind and juice of ½ lemon
1-2 tablespoons yoghurt or
  milk if necessary to make
  the mixture sufficiently
  moist

Beat together the margarine and honey until thick and pale, then beat in the eggs, flour, wheatgerm and baking powder. Add all the other ingredients and mix. A little yoghurt or milk may be needed to make a dropping consistency, but this will depend on the type of fruits used.

Put into a greased, lined tin and bake on the centre shelf at No.3, 325°F, for about 1¾ hours or until firm.

*This is a very good cake, with excellent nutritional content. Store in the fridge.*

# *Index*

175

quick pizza 106

raisins
carrot, celery and raisin salad 73
nut and raisin yoghurt 161
ratatouille 138
raw root salad 74
red cabbage, sweet 63
rice, brown 15, 21, 116
and nut mould 127
and sunflower seed stuffing 149, 151, 153
recipe 146
cheese and rice stuffing 148, 149, 152
recipe 146
Chinese 124-5
creamy rice and apricot dessert 162
main meal savoury rice 118
salad 71
savoury rice with herbs 117
spicy chick peas with 125
tomato savoury rice 117
rolls
fresh for breakfast 167
soft brown 167
roughage in diet 12, 29-30
rye 21, 119

salad Niçoise 69
salads 65-79
salt 16
sauces, recipes for
aubergine and tomato 113
basic white 89
cheese 89
curry 120
egg 90
Italian tomato 112
mushroom 89
onion 90
parsley 90
piquant yoghurt 87
sweet herbal yoghurt 86
tomato 90
wine 91
yoghurt sunflower-seed 91
savoury French roll 77
scones, wholemeal 168
seeds 20
semolina, cheese soufflé with 112
semolina pudding 165
sesame and peanut butter biscuits 169
sesame seeds 20
shepherd's pie 135
side salads 71-9
skim milk powder 18, 29
slimmers, wholefood diet for 33-5
snacks 155-7
soufflés 110-11

soups 93-7
soya bean(s) 19
loaf 131
savoury 131
soya nut pancakes with creamed mushrooms 110
soya pancakes, enriched 106
spaghetti, sauces for 112-13
Spanish omelette 110-11
spinach 61-2
lasagne 114
noodles and cheese 115-16
pancakes 108
with spinach and curd cheese 108
quiche 101-2
savoury au gratin 142-3
split peas 19
dahl 122-3
green split pea salad 76
green split pea soup 94
sponge cakes 170
spreads
creamy peanut butter 83
curd cheese spread with pineapple and nuts 83
egg and cottage cheese 84
Liptauer cheese 82
starches 22, 28
stir fried vegetables 62
strawberry yoghurt 162
stuffings for vegetables 145-7
sugar 13-14, 22, 28, 37-8
and starch/fruit combinations 39
sunflower seeds 20
peanut and sunflower seed pudding 133
rice and sunflower seed stuffing 149, 151, 153
recipe 146
yoghurt sunflower-seed sauce 91
sweetcorn
corn and chick pea crumble 129
corn, millet and nut bake 127
pancake filling with 110
quiche 102

tabbouleh 78
tandoori dip 81
Textured Vegetable Protein see TVP
tomato(es)
and nut stuffing 150, 152
recipe 145
and onion stuffing 147, 150
recipe 145
aubergine and tomato crumble 139-40
aubergine and tomato sauce 113
cheese, onion and tomato quiche 100-1
cucumber and tomato salad 72
gazpacho (soup) 96